LEGENDS OF THE
CAIRNGORMS

AFFLECK GRAY

MAINSTREAM
PUBLISHING

First published in 1987 by
MAINSTREAM PUBLISHING COMPANY
(EDINBURGH), LTD.
7 Albany Street
Edinburgh EH1 3UG

ISBN 1 85158 072 7 (cloth)
ISBN 1 85158 067 0 (Pbk)

British Library Cataloguing in Publication Data
Gray, Affleck
    Legends of the Cairngorms
    1. Legends——Scotland——Cairngorms
    I. Title

    398.2'2'094124.   GR145.C3

    ISBN 1-85158-072-7 (Cloth)
    ISBN 1-85158-067-0 (Pbk)

Cover photograph by Douglas Corrance
Cover design by James Hutcheson

Typeset in 11 point Baskerville by Pulse Origination, Edinburgh.
Printed in Great Britain by Collins, Glasgow

LEGENDS OF THE CAIRNGORMS

For my Grandchildren
Alan John, Kenneth Neil and David Martin Robertson, Kingussie.
Lisa Michelle Gray, Sydney, Australia.

And my great nephew and great niece
Bruce Alexander and Carloyn Louise Gray, Coquitlam, B.C. Canada.

Contents

Foreword

By the Hon. Sir William A. Macpherson of Cluny and Blairgowrie, T.D.

AS 27th Chief of the Clan Macpherson I have the greatest pleasure in writing a foreword to Affleck Gray's *Legends of the Cairngorms*. Our Clan's lands were in earlier days largely astride the upper waters of the Spey, and close to the sites and scenes of many of the legends.

Many Clansmen and Clanswomen will have heard some of the legends. To those who have, and to those who have not, the tales of the White Horse of Spey, the Invertromie Giant, the Black Officer, and so many others will be both stirring and exciting, and will recall the places and the atmosphere of Badenoch, the Cairngorms and the other Highland areas to which they relate.

Our Clan is now spread about the world, but the magnetism of Badenoch and the Highlands is permanent and strong. It is an experience and a thrill to remember those lands and read these collected legends.

We owe a great debt to Affleck Gray, a native of the district, who has spent much of his life in the Highlands and who has collected together this fascinating set of legends, inspired by his love of the district, his love for an old tale, and pride in his Badenoch Macpherson ancestry.

Too often Highlanders expect the old tales to be passed on and to survive without writing them down. Too many of the legends have thus been lost or have faded. Affleck Gray has indeed done a service to those of us who cherish the Highlands and wish to preserve for our children the feel, the sounds and the magic of the past in these hard lands.

As Chief of one of the great Clans of Badenoch and of the Spey I have much pleasure in recommending Affleck Gray's collection.

Introduction

THERE are few places in the Scottish Highlands richer in legendary lore than the valleys which lie in the shadow of the Cairngorms. It is, however, unfortunate that so many of the old tales, which were never recorded but handed down orally from generation to generation, have been completely lost since modern forms of entertainment superseded the old time ceilidhs. These tales are an essential part of the folk-tradition of the Highlands, and it is regrettable that so little has been done to perpetuate those of Upper Strathspey and Badenoch. The School of Scottish Studies, rather surprisingly, largely ignored the district apart from a few recordings by the late Dr. Calum Maclean in 1951-52.

As far as I know there has been no attempt hitherto to recover from near oblivion and record the tales which remain. I have for long cherished the idea of an anthology, probably inspired by the tales of Donald Macpherson, my grandfather, whose roots were in Badenoch; my love for the district in which I was born and bred, and my love for an old tale. It has been a long and time-consuming journey through an enchanted landscape peopled with fascinating characters. Ghosts did haunt, and giants did walk: they were a reality to the people, and reflect intrinsic forces in the hidden nature of the Highlands.

No doubt many of the tales in their long descent through successive ages have been distilled and redistilled by the poetical imaginations of the narrators, and have been subjected to considerable alteration and exaggeration. That is excusable, and the tales are no less palatable to those who love an old story. Some may seem so improbable that it may well be argued that they have no foundation in fact, but surely no legend, however improbable, could have been created without having at least some relevance to fact. What does seem inexcusable is the practice of some modern writers to pick up legends as they have been handed down, and dramatise them beyond all recognition.

Now that the task has been completed it gives me much pleasure to present this collection of tales in the hope that they will provide interest and entertainment to many who love the old legends of our fathers.

The legends commence at the south end of the district and move northwards through Badenoch, Rothiemurchus and Abernethy to Grantown-on-Spey, and finally to the foothills of the Cairngorms on the Mar side.

The Wife of Ben a' Ghlo

Now she flies high, now she flies low
And she lights on the summit of Ben a' Ghlo

TWO poachers from Braemar, Donald Gruer and Big John MacHardy, were hunting deer in the vicinity of Ben a' Ghlo one winter's day when they were overtaken by a sudden snow storm. When it cleared they stalked a hind, but only succeeded in wounding it. The trail of blood was easy to follow, but before they could come up with the poor beast a blinding blizzard from the north resulted in their losing all sense of direction. They turned their backs to the wind and struggled on in the approaching darkness, hoping to gain shelter in Glen Tilt. Suddenly a small, but unknown, glen appeared before them, and they decided to find out what shelter it might afford.

A small bothy loomed up in the gloom, and when they reached it the door was opened by an old woman who greeted them kindly enough, and said that they were not unexpected. She was tall and gaunt with long black hair and sunken eyes.

In spite of their exhaustion from cold and hunger, and gratitude to be out of the storm, the hunters sensed that there was something uncanny about this surprising encounter. To add to their unease the old woman chanted weird songs. Waving her arms, she would break into peals of eldritch laughter. Now she held up a rope with three knots and cried: "If I loose the first a soft wind will blow to gladden the hunter's hearts; if I loose the second a strong blast will sweep over the hills; if I loose the third a terrific storm will arise that neither man nor beast will endure. The blast will scream down the corries, and this bare arm will guide the course of the storm as I sit on my throne of Craig Gower on the top of Ben a' Ghlo".

She set before the terrified hunters a fresh salmon, and told them that it was she who had brought about the storm, and guided their footsteps to the bothy. She upbraided them for bringing no venison, and made them solemnly promise that they would leave a fat hind for her at Fraser's Cairn in Atholl at midnight in the first Monday of every month during the hind season. "If you fail", she warned, "evil will befall you, and you will surely perish in the mountain wastes. Your bones will be picked by the eagles and the raven will croak your dirge".

Overcome with fatigue the hunters promised to do her bidding, and soon fell asleep. When they awoke at dawn the old hag had gone.

History does not record that the hunters carried out her bidding to the letter.

The Vampire of Fealar

THERE is an old bothy near Fealar at the foot of Ben a' Ghlo which poachers used when no one was about. In the early 1920's two poachers arrived at the bothy, but they found it locked, and so had to break a window to gain entry. A fire was lit and one of them started to climb back through the window to fetch water. He had only one leg over the sill when he began to scream that something was tearing his leg and sucking his blood. At last he freed himself, but he was in great pain and in a state of terror. They both then climbed out through the window and made a thorough search round the bothy, but all they could see was white winged objects and faint blue lights flitting to and fro in the distance. To re-enter they burst the door lock and cooked a meal. They were in such dread that they did not dare close an eye.

Next day they again examined the ground but could find nothing but their own footsteps. It is recorded that the man bore the mark of his injuries for the rest of his life. It is certain that they never again went near Fealar. The older inhabitants believed that the bothy was an evil place haunted by the "Vampire of Fealar".

The Great Worm of Drumochter

MICHAEL SCOTT, the celebrated Scottish Wizard, was born in Blawearie on Ettrick Water, and lived at Oakwood Tower near Selkirk in the 13th century. Sir Walter Scott introduces him in his 'Lay of the Last Minstrel', and by a poetical anachronism it appears as if the Wizard lived in the 17th century. Michael Scott studied abroad and earned fame for his breadth of learning. Tytler wrote, "the apparatus of his laboratory, the oriental costume worn by the astrologers of the times, and the appearance of the white haired and venerable sage as he sat on the roof of his tower observing the face of the heavens, and conversing with the stars, were all amply sufficient to impress the minds of the vulgar with awe and terror". His influence on the minds of the common people in the Borders was such that, according to Sir Walter Scott, any work of great antiquity is ascribed to the agency of Auld Michael, or Sir William Wallace, or of the Devil.

Towards the end of his life he retired to Oakwood Tower and when he died he was buried, it is believed, with his kindred at Melrose Abbey. His magic books were said to have been interred with him, but it was said that the fiends who guarded them prevented any attempt to retrieve them.

As a young man the Wizard once crossed over Drumochter with two young friends. As they approached Dalwhinnie they were attacked by a huge white worm and Michael's friends took to their heels. He boldly stood his ground, and after a fierce battle slew the loathsome creature. In the Inn at Dalwhinnie that night they spoke freely of their encounter with the dragonish worm which they had cut into three and carried with them.

The landlord, a notorious rogue, said that for the middle portion he would give them free lodgings for the night. Michael readily agreed, and the landlord bade his wife make broth with it. Curious to know what dragon broth tasted like, and quite innocent of any other motive, Michael rubbed his finger on the spoon that was being used for stirring the soup and sucked. Instantly his mind was enrichened with power and knowledge that it had not previously possessed; the language of the birds and beasts, command over the Devil himself, and much more besides. But he knew also that unwittingly he had stolen the powers of the dragon worm from the innkeeper and his host would certainly kill him is he could. So with his friends he speedily shook the dust of the Dalwhinnie Inn from his feet.

Many years later Michael, then an old man, returned to Drumochter. He was much enfeebled and his friends, knowing that he had nearly reached the end of the road, brought a priest to administer the last rites. When the priest learned the identity of the dying man he lifted his hands in horror and refused all succour, refused to listen to any confessions and exclaimed, "to Hell you belong, to Hell you will go". Opening his eyes Michael said in a weak but strong voice, "Hang my heart from the branch of a fir tree then hide and watch. If a raven carries it away the priest spoke true. If a dove comes you will know that I spoke truth when I claimed that my powers as a magician were used only for good, and that God has forgiven me for all my other sins".

Whereupon he gave up the ghost and his friends duly cut out his heart as they had promised. The heart was hung on the branch of a fir tree and soon a raven swooped down, but when it was about to clutch the heart in its claws the observer saw a strange flash of light pass between the heart and the bird. Frightened the raven flew swiftly away. Then a dove came and carried off the magician's heart.

The Devil was in a passion because he had already prepared a grave of white molten rock for Michael. It was said that the priest, too, was much perturbed.

The Clan Battle of Dalwhinnie

IN EARLY days meetings between the Northern Highland Chiefs and the more powerful Barons of the South were held at Dalwhinnie to make treaties or bargain over grievances. The name signifies "the meeting dell".

Sometimes these meetings ended in bloody affrays, and there is no lack of evidence that this was the case for over the years skeletons have been dug up and the mounds of certain graves could, until recently, be seen.

On one occasion a meeting was held between Lochiel and Murray of Atholl in connection with a boundary dispute. The wary Lochiel took the precaution of consulting a "*barr-fhaidh*", a notable female seer. Having explained the purpose of his meeting with Atholl he then asked her if he would succeed in his mission.

"No", she replied. "Trust not yourself unarmed near Atholl. He means to kill you".

"Nonsense", exclaimed Lochiel, "he has promised on his honour to come with only two attendants and I have agreed likewise".

"If you do, my Chief, you will not return alive to Lochaber; he is preparing to bring hundreds. Oh, Lochiel, be warned for I see into the future as you know, distrust Atholl, take with you a strong body of the clan".

The woman's reputation as a prophetess was so firmly established, and she was so solicitous for his safety, that Lochiel, despite himself, was impressed. Perhaps Atholl's intentions were indeed treacherous. So on the appointed day he was prepared for foul play by concealing two hundred of his clan in the heather near the meeting place. At a prearranged signal they were to come to his aid in the event of treachery.

With his two followers he preceeded to the meeting place where he found Atholl with only two followers. Conscience stricken, Lochiel inwardly upbraided himself for doubting his friend's honour, and vowed that the false seer would be hanged from the nearest tree on his return home. Now he approached Atholl with feelings of shame, and prayed that Atholl would not detect the presence of his clansmen. However, their greetings were amicable and they sat down to discuss the matter in dispute. Meanwhile the attendants stood a few paces behind.

Atholl wore a short, grey, red-lined cloak, and while they talked it continually slipped off his shoulders. On one occasion, as if by accident, he turned the inside out. Immediately Lochiel sprang up and glancing suspiciously round detected the heads of men appearing above the heather.

"Ha!," cried Lochiel, "what have we here?"

"Oh, just Atholl sheep come to eat Lochaber grass", answered Atholl standing up.

Lochiel stepped back and waved his bonnet. Immediately his clansmen swarmed from the heather. "Oh", cried Atholl "and what have we now?"

"Lochaber dogs come to worry Atholl's sheep. Draw you treacherous dog."

There was a bloody conflict and few Atholl men escaped the slaughter. The burial mounds were until quite recently to be seen on the West side of the railway bridge near the Hydro Electric Board workshop at Dalwhinnie, but extensive ploughing for afforestation was carried out in 1980 and, probably in ignorance of the significance of the mounds, the corner where they were situated was unfortunately also torn up and planted.

The Submerged Parish

IN OLDEN days it was believed that Loch Ericht was once a fertile, well-populated valley which in past ages disappeared in some awful cataclysm. According to tradition the long expanse of water reaching from near Dalwhinnie to Rannoch, a distance of approximately fourteen miles by an average of one-quarter of a mile wide, and covering an area of approximately 2240 acres was called *Sgir Eadail*, the Parish of Eadail. Eadail is a corruption of the Gaelic word '*feudail*' meaning wealth in cattle and the valley may have been well-named. The Rev. Thos. Sinton, author of the *Poetry of Badenoch* and other books, believed however, that the name Ericht or Errachd was derived from an entirely different source. "The ancient burial ground of Biallid (that is about one-quarter of a mile West of Newtonmore on the Laggan road) was called *Cladh Pheadal* or *Pheadailt* — both forms of the name being colloquial renderings of Peadar i.e. St. Peter."

It is alleged to have been the Churchyard connected with a prehistoric parish termed *Sgir Eadail*. Colloquially the strengthening 't' is often added to the name making it *Eadailt* or *Pheadailt*. According to legend this parish embraced the whole of Glen Truim and the valley of Loch Errachd including an extensive flat of good land now covered entirely by the water of that Loch. Mr. Sinton's views were published about 25 years before the Grampian Electricty Board built dams at each end of Loch Ericht, raising the level of the water and flooding the valley.

According to legend the cataclysm, if such there was, caused the destruction of everything in the valley. People, cattle, houses disappeared. It is even said that in clear weather the ruins of buildings can be seen at the bottom of the Loch, and on a calm evening the tolling of a church bell may be heard. In 1928, when the dam was being constructed at the Dalwhinnie end of the Loch by the Grampian Electricity Authority, the ancient bed of a river which ran towards the Truim was discovered. The conclusion reached then was that an upheaval of some nature had dammed the river and the water had ponded back and flooded the valley to some extent. The river now runs from the dam at the west end of the Loch and is called the Ericht or Eireachd.

I am grateful to Mr. G. Ronald Curtis, of the North of Scotland Hydro-Electric Board, for the following observations:

From the Bathymetrical Survey of 1900 it is known that the water level was 1153 feet above sea level; the south west part of the loch was just over 500 feet deep; the north west part of the loch was just over 300 feet deep; there was a shallow part 200 feet deep opposite Coire Bhachidh; and another shallow opposite Loch Ericht Lodge. At the south west end there was a considerable area of the loch which was very shallow, there is relatively flat land where the River Ericht emerges (its bed level being 1150 feet), and there are deposits of sand and gravel buried by deposits of peat. Ericht Dam was built over one mile further downstream than the natural outlet from the loch.

At the north east end the loch was also shallow and the valley is wide and flat. When Dalwhinnie Dam was built here the underlying strata were exposed. The ground surface was at 1167 feet and there was a thin level layer of peat across most of the area except near the north west side where the peat was 15 feet thick. Underlying the peat there is an extensive layer of sand and gravel, its surface being mostly level at about 1165 feet but having a hollow (peat filled) at a level of 1152 feet near the north west side of the valley, which indicates the existence of a low point, being possibly an extension of the loch or a river inlet or outlet. This would be in post-glacial and pre-peat times say 800-2000 BC.

Underlying this gravel there is rock whose surface slopes down from both sides of the valley to a low point near the centre at 1132 feet.

I think this would have been formed by the passage of ice at the height of the ice ages but it has been filled with the sand and

21

gravel either by direct ice action or by water as the ice retreated. The loch is on a very significant geological fault line running straight from upper Speyside to Loch Awe and beyond.

Obviously then, Loch Ericht could have been discharged in the opposite direction, i.e. to the Spey in earlier times (as did the River Tilt and Loch Awe for example). I think this is supported by the nature of the ditch which now flows north-east between Dalwhinnie Station and the Grampian Hotel. Such changes due to erosion of rivers etc. would have been slow and not catastrophic.

I can see the possibility of ancient earthquakes in this fault raising or lowering one end of the loch relative to the earth and causing changes in the flow and a tidal wave in the process but these actions are unlikely to have occurred in the last two millenia as they are not supported by historic evidence.

There remains the possibility of a catastrophe to a low lying village on the shore due to an earthquake causing a major landslide (Question: Is there evidence for this in aerial photographs?) and accompanying tidal wave; or hurricane winds causing 'set up' of the water surface at one end of such a long loch; and so on. The more I learn from myths the more I believe they contained truth but I find it very hard to find an explanation for a cataclysmic event in historical times, and impossible for the 16th century as required by the little gravestones.

Since the dams were built the top water level has been raised by 26 feet to 1179 feet above sea level but in extreme drought the actual water level is likely to fall to nearly its earlier level.

It is hardly proof of the legend because of the relatively recent date, but it is worth recording that when a man was fishing from an anchored boat at the west end of Loch Ericht he discovered when he pulled up his anchor that there was a small gravestone attached to it bearing the brief inscription, "Elspet Robertson; died 1545". Where it came from is a mystery. The Author is convinced that he saw the stone somewhere many years ago, but, cannot recall exactly where. It does not appear to be in any museum at which enquiries were made.

The Spectre of the Boar

HENRY TEGNER, author of a number of interesting books on the outdoors, including a valuable work on the ornithology of Strathspey, contributed an article to *Scotland's Magazine* in March 1963 in which he briefly discussed the Big Grey Man of Ben MacDhui. He expressed the view that when eminent men of science like Professor Collie and Dr Kellas bear witness to experiencing fear on Ben MacDhui it is difficult to doubt that something out of the ordinary does, in fact, appear on occasions in certain less frequented Highland locations.

Although Tegner had frequently walked through the Lairig Ghru, at all times of the year and in all sorts of weather, he had never experienced anything of an abnormal nature. But he was convinced of the Grey Man's existence for he had seen something remarkably like his double in another part of the Grampian range.

It happened long before the 1939-45 war when he was stalking in the Forest of Drumochter. Locally the phenomenon was known as the 'Spectre of the Boar', the Boar, or Boar of Badenoch, being the conical hill which towers above the Drumochter Pass on the A9 Perth-Inverness road.

One day in the month of October Tegner was out with Kennedy the stalker. They found no deer in Glen Tuirc, nor a sight of any on the slopes of Marcaonach. They spied the Boar and sighted a small herd of hinds with an old stag lying well above them. The ground was fairly easy, and weather conditions favourable with a steady wind from the south-west. When they started there was little sunshine and a good deal of low cloud. Occasionally wisps of mist trailed over the summits of the Boar, and the Sow of Atholl further south. The stalk was not likely to present any difficulties.

They crossed the Tuirc burn, leaving the ghillie in a concealed spot near the base of the Boar, and by working their way up one of the little burns were able to get well above their quarry. Meanwhile the wind appeared to be strengthening as they stalked to within a quarter of a mile of the stag. The clouds began to disperse and glimpses of blue sky were revealed through rents in the mist. Trailing wisps swept across the face of the Boar.

They rested momentarily, and just as they stirred to resume Tegner's eye caught a movement towards the summit of the Boar. He scanned the ground with his telescope but he could see nothing. Then the sun broke through a gap in the clouds and he saw the 'thing' moving quite distinctly just below the skyline above them.

Tapping Kennedy on the shoulder he whispered to him to look above, but again there was nothing to be seen. The deer remained grazing peacefully. Yet Tegner was positive that his imagination had not misled him, and as they moved on he had the growing conviction that they were being followed. Suddenly he knew that his eyes had not been deceived:

"The figures were huge as they appeared to travel at great speed across a long streak of mist which enveloped the skyline of the Boar of Badenoch. This time I was certain, I was not dreaming.

'There's someone above us, Kennedy,' I said.

Kennedy stopped to look towards the figures. He saw them, and his jaw dropped whilst his eyes stared. The figures were standing now as if they were looking down at us. They appeared like two giants gazing down on two dwarfs. They did not seem to be much more than a hundred yards from where we stood. It was an extra-ordinary experience seeing those great figures out there on the hillside. It was certainly uncanny and I felt myself shiver although that day was not unduly cold.

Kennedy was obviously upset by what he had seen. As we stared up into the mist-laden face of the hill the figures quickly disappeared as if they had climbed out of our sight.

'It's the Spectre we've been seeing,' said Kennedy. He

shook his head in that meaning way which somehow portends disaster. We waited for a few minutes to recover our composure. I was the first to use my glasses to look for the deer we were after. They were nowhere to be seen. Whether the Spectre had put them away, or whether it was our own carelessness I shall never know."

The ghillie told them later that he had seen nothing except the deer suddenly moving off at speed towards the ridge of Marcaonach. Tegner had this to say in conclusion:

"In retrospect I believe what we saw that day on the Boar of Badenoch was a trick of sun and cloud such as happens when one is in an aircraft when the shadow of the plane is cast on a cloud band. The machine in strong silhouette appears to be travelling fast across a backdrop of clouds. The sun could well have cast our shadows - Kennedy's and mine - on to the wreaths of mist above us on the slopes of the Boar of Badenoch."

If such is a proper interpretation of the Spectre then this may well explain the Grey Man of Ben MacDhui, and other Grampian 'ghosts' as well. But then, of course, I may well be wrong. I hope so, anyway, as such things as the Grey Man, the Spectre, and the Monster of Loch Ness make pleasant additions to the romantic Highland scene.

The Macphersons of Crubenmor always regarded the Boar as their supernatural home, and if Mr. Tegner had lived in Badenoch in a by-gone age he may have arrived at a different conclusion. He would have been told that what he had witnessed was the ghost of Duncan Macpherson, one of the old Crubenmor Chieftains and his ghillie. Once in a while they were wont to appear suddenly through the mist, and may still do so.

The Battle of Invernahavon

THE site of the Battle was at the confluence of the Truim and the Spey. It was about the year 1370 when the Camerons from Lochaber entered Badenoch to plunder the lands of the MacIntoshes and Macphersons with whom they were constantly at war. They were met and opposed by the MacIntoshes, Macphersons and the Clan Daidh (Davidsons), a small but powerful Clan whose ancestral home was near the site. They were slaughtered to such an extent in this battle that their losses were never recovered, and they almost disappeared from their ancestral lands. Before the fight the Macphersons claimed their traditional right of holding the right wing.

When, however, they were told that the honour had been bestowed on Clann 'ic Dhaidh they were so infuriated by this seeming insult that they withdrew, crossed the Spey, and on a knoll north of the confluence of the two rivers they sat calmly munching bannocks, watching the clash of arms below. They saw the Camerons overwhelming the Macintoshes and Davidsons. The Chief of the Davidsons and seven sons fell mortally wounded in sight of their home.

The Macintoshes were already being routed, but still the Macphersons remained aloof and disdainful until the Macintosh Chief in desperation prevailed upon his former allies to support him by a cunning stratagem. Summoning his bard he commanded him to compose a satire on the Macphersons, taunting them with pusillanimous conduct before their hereditary enemy, and to deliver and recite it to Cluny Macpherson himself. He was further commanded to tell Cluny that he had been sent by Lochiel, not the Macintosh.

The office of bard in those days was very senior, and he was always given the greatest respect. He had no difficulty in passing the Macpherson guards and gaining an audience of the Chief whose indulgence he begged in listening to his lay. Believing that the taunts of cowardice flung at him came from Lochiel, the Chief rose in fury, and calling his clan to arms set out in pursuit of the victorious Camerons who were by now drawing westwards in the twilight of a May night. The enemy were encamped beyond Phoiness at Dalanach, and the Macphersons immediately attacked.

Careless in the afterglow of victory the Camerons were taken by surprise, and the sudden onslaught of the Macphersons proved disastrous for them. One leader after another was lost in the running fight as the Camerons retreated westwards, and they were all but spent when Loch Patag was reached.

Not far from Loch Patag, at Dail an Lungart on Loch Ericht side, the epic duel between two renowned bowmen, *MacDhomhnuill Dhuibh* (Son of Black Donald) Chief of the Camerons, and one of the Macpherson leaders known as *MacIain Ceann Dubh* (Son of John of the Black Head), took place. Despite the differences which existed between their respective clans they were friends, and when the historic duel began Macpherson called out to his opponent as he drew his bow *"Tharam 's tharad, a Thearlaich"* (over me and over you Charles). As the arrow flew over him Cameron at once understood the message, and in his turn shot his arrow over Macpherson's head. Unfortunately the arrows mortally wounded a number of the onlookers, and when the Chief of the Macphersons saw his men lying dead behind MacIain he raged at the bowman. "Where is your old skill Ceann Dubh? Surely your mother was a Cameron".

Stung by the taunt MacIain called to his friend *"Uman 's umad, a Thearlaich"* (For me and for you Charles). Both now fired their arrows in earnest, and each fell mortally wounded. At Dail an Lungart on the side of Loch Ericht there was, and may still be, a moss-covered cairn marking the spot where the Cameron fell. It was called Carn Mhic Dhomhnuill Duibh.

The White Lady of the Rowan Tree

THERE is a bridge in Glentruim near a sharp bend on the glen road. An old rowan tree with a rotten heart in which bees were wont to swarm and work, and provide the people who knew with honey, used to stand there, but it has long since fallen with decay. When the moon was full the people of the district would not pass the dreaded spot. Even the horses refused to cross the bridge, but of their own accord would go lower down stream and ford the river. Even dogs howled mournfully at something the human eye could not discern, although a few old people claimed to have seen a ghost-like figure in white raiment, and with outstretched arms standing beside the big rock at the bridge.

Tradition has it that a certain local worthy took a bet to cross the bridge on the night of dread. Well fortified with John Barleycorn he approached the bridge on horseback, but when the animal stopped short of the bridge and refused to budge he stumbled over the bridge on foot past the rowan tree. There, at the base of the rock, he came face to face with the White Lady. What happened no-one knows, but the next day he was found in a ditch about a quarter of a mile further along the road, his face in a pool of water. His horse was grazing quietly nearby.

The incident created so much talk in the country that one man more curious than all the others determined to keep a watch on the bridge at the next full moon. He moved silently to a spot a discrete distance from the bridge, and hid; nothing stirred. All of a sudden his blood froze in his veins; the rock was lit up with a brilliant white light, and there in front of him with outstretched arms was the figure of the woman. Rigid

28

with terror he watched for about five minutes until the light and the figure had vanished. Hastily, the observer made for home.

Alan of the Spoils

NEAR the East end of Loch Laggan lie the venerable ruins of St. Kenneth's Chapel. There is a curious tradition connected with the building of the Church, which was built by Alan Cameron, of the Lochiel family.

Alan, or *Ailean nan Creach* (Alan of the Spoils) as he was popularly called, was a noted freebooter who had a long series of successes in raiding his neighbour's cattle. But his luck ran out, and he encountered one disastrous raid after another. In order to counter his run of misfortunes Alan decided to attempt communication with the other world in the hope of discovering the reason for his failures.

There was a celebrated witch in his neighbourhood called *Gorm Shuil* (blue-eyed) and so adept was she in her profession that in a moment she could transform herself and others into hares and crows, raise gales and blizzards, and perform many other strange feats. Under her direction Alan took a cat, and along with a servant went one night to a corn kiln near Torcastle in Strathlochy. The cat was tied to a spit, and the servant commenced to roast it alive over a low fire, while Alan stood guard with drawn sword at the entrance. As soon as the poor cat commenced to screetch in agony a whole troop of cats gathered to attempt its rescue, but Alan kept them at bay. " '*S olc an carabh sin*" (that is a bad way to treat a cat) screamed the cats.

Alan said, "It will not be bettered just now", and kept repeating to his servant, "Whatever you may hear or see keep on turning the cat."

Then a huge one-eyed tom cat called *Cam Dubh* came forward, and calmly remonstrated with Alan for his cruelty, and told him that his reverses were all due to his wickedness in plundering his neighbours and to atone for his sins he must build seven churches, a church for each of his seven creachs. If he did not desist immediately *Cam Dubh*'s brother, "*Cluasa Leabhra mo bhrathair* (my brother with the long hanging ears) would take such vengence upon him that he would never receive again mercy from his Maker."

So sobering was the effect on Alan that he at once ordered his servant to release the cat, and lost no time in departing before the dreaded *Cluasa Leabhra* arrived.

In a fever of impatience he commenced building the first of the churches as directed by *Cam Dubh*, and before he died seven churches in all were constructed. One of these, it is said, was the old church of Laggan.

There used to be two islands in Loch Laggan but the level of the loch was raised in the 1920's to generate electricity for the aluminium factory at Fort William. But in dry weather, when the loch is drawn down, they reveal themselves again. On *Eilean an Righ* (the King's Island) King Fergus (c. 330 B.C.) is believed to have had a hunting lodge. He, along with four other early Kings of Scotland, are said to be buried in the present garden of Ardverikie on the south shore of the loch, but according to history King Fergus was lost at sea off a point on the west coast of Ireland ever since called Carrick Fergus. He had ruled Scotland and Ireland for twenty five years.

The other island, *Eilean nan Coin* (the Dogs' Island) is where the deer hounds were kennelled.

Round about 1940 when Loch Laggan was particularly low the remains of an ancient canoe were found in the mud near the shore.

The ruins of St. Kenneth's Chapel, one of the seven churches built by Alan, may be seen near the east end of the loch.

Another of his churches is *Cille Choirill* near the march between Brae Lochaber and Badenoch. It was restored in the early part of this century. The chapel bell has a musical tone and inside the air is fragrant with the scent of the pine timbers.

There is an ancient burial ground near the chapel. Here lies the dust of some of Brae Lochaber's illustrious sons including that of the renowned, immortal bard Iain Lom whom Charles II created Poet Laureate about 300 years ago. In 1900, or thereabout, a stone was erected to his memory beside the Chapel but older people at the time contended that his actual place of internment was higher up the slope, and that the stone is erected over the dust of another Lochaber bard, *Domhnull MacFhionnlaigh nan Dan* (Donald MacFinlay of the Poems).

Perhaps ironically *Ailean nan Creach* was sometimes called *Ailean nan Eaglais* (Alan of the Churches).

After being in a ruinous state for centuries *Cille Chorill* was restored through the generosity of Dr. John F. MacMaster and other descendents of Lochaber emigrants to Nova Scotia in the late 18th and early 19th centuries. It was formally opened in July 1932 by Bishop Alexander MacDonald of Victoria B.C., another emigrant descendent. An excellent history of *Cille Choirill* has been published by Ann MacDonell F.S.A. Scot and Robert MacFarlane. The proceeds from sales are intended for the fabric fund of the Church.

The Witch of Laggan

A MAN of Badenoch, noted for his hatred of witchcraft, was on a particular occasion stalking deer in the Forest of Gaick when a violent storm arose, and he had to seek shelter in his hunting bothy. His gun rested in a corner, but his *sgian dubh* (black knife carried in stocking) was at hand. His two deerhounds lay at his feet. The storm of wind and rain raged outside.

Suddenly a wretched cat entered the bothy. The dogs growled, bristling to attack. The cat entreated the hunter to restrain them, claiming that she was only a poor old witch who had mended her ways, and as a result had been sorely mistreated by the sisterhood. As a last resort she had fled to him for protection.

The hunter believed what she said for, to a man of his character, it was unthinkable to take advantage of an enemy in such circumstances. With some difficulty he quietened his dogs, and invited the cat to come to the fire and warm herself.

"Nay", said the cat, "if I do those furious hounds of yours will tear my poor hands to pieces; I pray you, therefore, take this long hair and tie the dogs therewith to the beam of the house that I may be secure from their molestation."

The hunter took the hair, and leading the dogs aside he pretended to bind them as he was directed; instead he bound the hair round the beam which supported the roof of the bothy. The cat then came and squatted in front of the fire, but immediately she began to grow and grow, and the hunter remarked jocularly, "An evil death to you nasty beast; you are getting very large."

"Aye, aye", said the cat equally jocose, "as my hairs dry in the heat they naturally expand." She grew and grew until she was as big as a deerhound when, in a twinkling, she turned into a woman, and to the hunter's horror the form of a good neighbour whom he had long known by the name of The Good Wife of Laggan: a woman regarded by all in that district as a very paragon of virtue. "Hunter of the hills", she cried "your hour has come; the day of reckoning has arrived; long have you been the devoted enemy of my persecuted sisterhood. The chief aggressor against our order is now no more. This morning I saw his body consigned to a watery grave; and now hunter of the hills it is your turn." Whereupon, she flew at him like a tigress, but the dogs she supposed to be securely tied up flew at her face and breast in turn. In terror she cried out addressing the hair that was supposed to be tying the dogs to the rafter, "Fasten hair, fasten", and so effectively did the hair obey the order that it snapped the beam in two.

Seeing herself deceived, the witch tried to escape but the dogs clung to her breast, and only released their hold when all their teeth fell out, but not before one of her breasts was almost severed, and now with a fearful shriek she assumed the likeness of a raven, and flew off in the direction of her home. The dogs were so spent that all they could do was lick their master's hand before expiring at his feet. Sorrowfully he remained only long enough to bury his faithful companions, before setting out for home in a state of perplexity and wonder.

When he arrived his wife was absent, but she soon appeared and told him that she had been visiting the Good Wife of Laggan who was unwell with a severe colic, brought on by a chill contracted that day at a peat moss. She was so ill that all the neighbours felt she would not recover.

"Aye, aye," her husband remarked, "it is proper that I also should go and see her."

Having reached the house, and the bedside of the witch where all the neighbours were lamenting her imminent demise, he immediately whipped off the bedcovers and cried "Behold the object of your solicitude! This morning she was a party to the death of John Garve MacGille Chalum of Raasay, and today she attempted to make me share his doom; but the arm of providence has overtaken the servant of Satan in her career, and she is now about to expiate her crimes by death in this world, and punishment in the next." The company was seized with consternation, but who could question the truth of what the hunter said when they beheld the marks on her person. Nor did the witch deny anything he had said. In penitent tones she addressed herself to her neighbours.

"My dear and respected friends spare, oh spare, an old neighbour while in the agonies of death and greater mortal degradation. Already the enemy of your souls and minds who seduced me from the walks of virtue and happiness as a reward for my anxious and increasing labours in his service only waits to lead my soul into the eternal punishment, and as a warning to all others to shun the awful rock on which I have split. I shall detail to you means and artifices by which I was led into the services of the evil one, and the treachery which I and all others have experienced at his hands."

She related the particulars of the means by which Satan had seduced her, and the various adventures on which she had been engaged, concluding with the death of Raasay that very day, and her attack on the hunter. Then, with the most agonising shriek, she died.

The same night there was a sequel to her death. Two travellers crossing the Monadh Liath from Strathdearn to Badenoch were terrified by the sudden appearance of a woman running at full tilt towards Strathdearn. Her bosom and front was covered with blood, and as she ran she emitted the most appalling shrieks. She had no sooner disappeared from sight than two black dogs appeared, obviously following her scent. Then they met a black man on a black horse who demanded, "Did you meet a woman as you came over the hills?"

The travellers said they had. "Did you meet two dogs tracking the woman?" asked the horseman. "We did indeed", said the travellers.

"Well", said the black rider, "do you think the dogs would have caught her before she reached the churchyard at Dalarossie?"

"Well", said the travellers, "they would at any rate be very close on her heels." With that the horseman dug his spurs into the black horse and galloped off at a furious speed.

Before they emerged from the Forest of Monadh Liath they were overtaken by the black rider; the body of the woman lay across the bow of his saddle; one dog clung to her breast, the other to her thigh.

When the travellers at last reached habitation, and recounted their frightening experience, no one doubted that the mutilated figure they had encountered was the spirit of the witch racing to reach the churchyard at Dalarossie, which was well known to be sacred ground, and a sanctuary for those dead or alive from the bondage of Satan. It seemed that the Good Wife of Laggan's turn of speed was just not enough.

The Witch of Badenoch

WHEN the Comyns were Lords of Badenoch the Chief took it into his head to build a castle of such dimensions and strength that it could never be breached or destroyed by human hands. Instead of employing masons he enlisted the services of the notorious Witch of Badenoch who, for a large sum of gold, agreed to transport stones to the site he had chosen and build an impregnable fortress with the magic of her own hands.

First she searched for two similar enormous boulders for doorposts on the outer gate, but in the whole length and breadth of Scotland she could not find a pair to suit her purpose. She began to despair until she met a sister witch from the Isle of Man, to whom she confessed her dilemma. Her sister witch calmed her fears, and described two matching stones at a place on the Manx Hills. So she flew to the Isle of Man, and without difficulty found the stones.

She lifted one and put it in her apron, and in brilliant moonlight set off on her return journey to Badenoch. At dawn she was high above Glenfernate, just when a hunter was returning to Atholl with the haunches of a deer on his back. On seeing the great black mass flying through the air he dropped the haunches and in astonishment cried out *"Dhia gleidh sinn"* (God bless us). The utterance of the holy name instantly destroyed the witch's power. Her apron strings snapped, and the great boulder fell to earth and rolled down to the bottom of Glenfernate where it rests to this day. It is called *Clach Mór* or the Witch's Stone. Twenty feet high and seventy-four feet in circumference, it is estimated to weigh one thousand tons. There is no other rock of this kind in the district, and the scientific explanation is that in an early

37

glacial period it had been iceborn from a distant land. But the old folk knew better than that.

The Witch could never after this get apron strings to hold even small boulders, and the dream castle of the Comyn was never built. Tradition says, that on the anniversary the Witch returns and works from sunset until dawn trying to move the *Clach Mór*, and for a long time people gave the unhallowed spot a wide berth on that particular night.

The Witch of Nuide

THERE was a time when the people in the vicinity of Nuide, Ruthven, Milton and Riverton lived in terror of a witch who lived near Nuide House. Such was their dread of her that they regularly paid her tribute in money, or kind; those who defied her power paid dearly in cows going dry, stock dying mysteriously, and even buildings going up in flames. They lived in such a state of trepidation that they even feared to go from home by horse or cart, or occupy any position of importance in the community without begging her leave.

In the course of time a new tenant came to Ruthven from the Lowlands who scoffed at witchcraft and treated the witch with contempt and defiance, refusing to pay her a penny. But one evening when he was watching the cattle in one of the meadows near Ruthven Castle along with his herd he spied a hare going round the cows sucking their milk. "Well", he said in astonishment, "I would have believed that of a hedgehog but never of a hare. I will shoot it."

He carried a gun and creeping in on the hare he fired both barrels right into it. To his dismay the hare scampered away, then sat down on its haunches and simply gazed at him without fear. Later the herd boy said that the hare put a forefoot to its nose and jeered! Be that as it may there is no doubt that every cow touched by the hare went dry. The farmer was certainly puzzled, but refused to believe that the witch had anything to do with it. He blamed a certain weed, and the cows were moved to another pasture, but to no purpose. One after another they became sick and died, and much against the grain he began to think seriously about the witch's powers. To appease her he sent the herd to her cottage with two fat ducks saying, "Take that to the old hag and may they choke her."

The offering was sternly refused. "Tell your master I fear they would choke me, but by the end of the next moon I will choke him."

Soon after when he was returning from a fair at Newtonmore in torrential rain which had swollen the Spey and made it unfordable, the farmer had to go round by Ralia bridge and walk home by Nuide. The night was dark and stormy; his only companions two collies. After crossing Inverton Burn the dogs suddenly came to his right side growling fiercely. Faintly in the poor light he made out the form of a huge greyhound on his left. He had barely time to raise his stick before the beast was at his throat. There was a fearful struggle but at last the brute was driven off screaming with the two collies hanging on to its flanks. Then the farmer heard an agonised cry, "Call back your dogs, call back your dogs", but even if he had been willing he was too exhausted to pay attention. Neither the witch nor the dogs were ever seen in Badenoch again and the people rejoiced.

The Horses of Spey

THE Spey is an eccentric river; it seldom chuckles or wimples, but it often grumbles and roars. Like a woman, whose strength of character is more obvious than her beauty, it gains in respect and fear what it may lose in admiration. Many, over the years, neglected to pay it respect and consequently lost their lives. There was a saying that her waters demanded at least one life a year, and in that respect Spey was perhaps less greedy than the Dee of which it was said:

Blood-thirsty Dee,
Each year it needs three.

Or the Till in the Lowlands:

Said Tweed tae Till
"Whit gars ye rin sae still?"

Till said tae Tweed
"Tho ye rin wi' speed
An I rin slaw
Whaur ye droon ae man
I droon twa."

Little wonder that in olden days the people who lived close to Spey believed in an evil spirit that lurked in its depths — *An t-Each Ban* (The White Horse). White horses figure frequently in Celtic faerie tales but the colour is unusual for the *Each Uisge* (Water Horse or Kelpie) is usually black. In all other respects, however, the handsome beast that emerged from Spey behaved in the traditional manner. Most frequently it was to be encountered on stormy nights when clouds raced across the sky, and, hiding the moon one moment, threw the

41

countryside into gloom; the next moment flooding it with the silver light that brings into relief every branch and twig. The unwary traveller picking his way wearily towards his destination might suddenly find the great horse at his side; sleek, daintily stepping, clad in the finest trappings; whinnying softly, nuzzling the traveller's hand with his velvet nose, the eyes gentle and questioning. Here to the traveller was a heaven-sent gift for his weariness, and a speedy way of reaching his journey's end. But woe to him! Once mounted he knew instantly that his fate was sealed. With a hideous scream the white horse broke into a furious gallop, his mane and tail streaming in the rushing wind. Terror stricken the rider was powerless to break the spell that bound him to the creature's back, and then, with a great leap from the bank, it plunged into the deep pool it knew so well leaving nothing but a scream of triumph for yet another victim to devour.

In the deep pools of Spey a yellow horse also had its abode. At one time it carried away only girls, then changed its habits and took married couples. It was always on the alert, and as soon as it saw a couple standing on the bank seeking to find a way of fording the river he would sidle up to them and gently nuzzle them, and offer to convoy them across. But as soon as they mounted he would plunge into the nearest pool and devour them.

Curiously all highland water horses appear to have been richly caparisoned. In human form their dress was often dandified, but usually they wore homespun clothes of an old fashioned design. It was said that if a woman could have got her hands on one of the richly embellished bridles, and replaced it with a cow shackle she could have dominated the *each uisge* for the rest of her life, and the bridle would have brought her good fortune. But only a woman could have done this, and there is no record of such an achievement.

Cluny's Cave

NO Highland Chief emerged in history from the troubled years of the 1745 Rebellion with such a record of integrity and faithfulness as Ewan Macpherson, popularly called Ewan Ban, the Son of the Chief of the Macpherson Clan. His adventures following Culloden are a saga in itself.

His estates were confiscated, and butcher Cumberland saw to it that Cluny Castle was burned to the ground. But Ewan's lady was left unmolested, and with Cumberland's gracious permission she was allowed to stay in a small house near the Castle. Here Ewan stole occasionally despite the vigilance of Cumberland's soldiers. There was a recess in the wall in which he concealed himself when danger threatened, and though there was a price of one thousand pounds on his head not one of his faithful clan ever fell for the wiles of the soldiers who were desperate for his capture. He lived nine years succoured by his people, warned of every move the soldiers made. So faithful were they that for the rest of his life they paid two rents, an almost intolerable burden, one perforce to the Government, the other to their Chief.

Cluny's principal hiding place was a cave on the face of Creag Dhubh about three miles from Cluny Castle. It is high on the face of the steep, rocky, birch-clad hill from which the Macphersons took their war cry, "Creag Dhubh, creag dhubh". It is small and requires agility to reach it. The cave is gained by following a narrow ledge across the face of the hill with a steep drop below. Where the ledge ends there is a drop to the mouth of the cave where a large stone is set, making the entrance more difficult to detect. One has to stoop to enter, but once inside, it is remarkably roomy, and a suitable haven for two or three men. Half way along the cave there is a small 'window' near the roof, which was no doubt constantly manned. At the back of the cave a second narrow opening appears to have been the vent for a hearth which was a broad ledge a little above floor level. A commanding view of the valley below can be seen from it. It was probably from here that Ewan Ban saw his home consumed by fire; perhaps he wondered about the Green Banner of Clan Chattan with which the fortunes of the clan are inexorably connected, and the Fairy Chanter which dropped from heaven to inspire the clan to deeds of valiance and endurance.

The cave was excavated by the clan who worked during the night and deposited the spoil in Lochan Ovie below so well that not a trace of the operation could be seen. Here Cluny lived securely, although a hundred people knew the location of his hideout. Here he received night visits from his friends who brought food, drink and information.

Other retreats were prepared in case the military became suspicious and he had to flee. The most remarkable of these was known as Cluny's Cage, a cave on Ben Alder. It was here that he entertained Prince Charles in his last dire distress, and told him of the ship that was ready to carry him from Scotland. Not long after, Cluny himself escaped to France, where he died a year later.

Down by the Spey are the remains of a second retreat, a subterranean dwelling from which sand and gravel were excavated in the dead of night to avoid suspicion. There is a tradition that Cluny, when in hiding here, was surprised one day when the roof collapsed and a stranger fell in beside him. He grappled with him and felt for his dirk, but Cluny relented and asked the man, as a price for his life, if he would swear on oath never to reveal his hiding place to any man. The man of course swore willingly, but he was no sooner gone than Cluny began to doubt his own judgement and soon left the spot for a third retreat in the old house of Dalchully. It did not surprise him, knowing the price the Government had set on his head, to discover that the Redcoats had soon raided his subterranean home.

Eighty soldiers were permanently stationed in the district to intimidate the clansmen and try to force them to reveal their chief's hiding place. In addition to this other soldiers searched the glens and hills unceasingly for the wanted man. But all their efforts were scorned by his devoted family.

Almost one hundred and forty years later Sandy MacDonald, a piper of renown and a trusted friend of the Macphersons of Glen Truim, was ferreting rabbits a short distance away from the subterranean hiding place. He had occasion to move aside some large stones and found underneath them six old claymores. The conclusion reached was that these were placed there for Cluny's defence in the event of discovery and danger of capture for undoubtedly a few of his clansmen would always have been near at hand.

He had a number of cells prepared so that, in order to baffle the vigilance of the Redcoats, he never spent too many nights in the one place nor have his people attract attention by going too often in any one direction.

One of the most secure retreats was at Dalchully, three miles west of Cluny Castle, where he was secure, dry and comfortable in a vault under the floor of the house. It measured about eight feet square and was entered by a trapdoor in the floor. When it was covered by a carpet there was no suspicion of its existence. It was linked with planks and because of the gravelly soil it was never damp. In later years it was used for storing cheeses. The vault remains to this day.

A short distance west of Dalchully, *Dun-da-lamh* occupies the summit of a large wooded knoll. It means the fort of the two hands, or two-handed, by reason of the low hill on the one side and a spur on the other about half its height. It has been described by an authority as "the most perfect relic of a British stronghold of the class in Britain." It is joined to the adjoining hills on the west side by a narrow neck of land about 100 feet lower than the Dun itself, and about 300 yards long. The adjacent hills are perhaps 200 to 300 feet higher. The inside measurements of the Dun are 420 feet long by 250 feet at the west end and 75 feet at the east end. The wall appears to have varied considerably in height and thickness. It is now from 2 to 5 feet high and 14 feet thick. At the west end there it is most exposed it is 17 feet thick and in the north west corner 25 feet thick. This is the easiest approach and the most vulnerable. The height of the wall here is still 13 feet high and appears to have been regarded as impregnable and has only been built up where there are gaps in the rocks. At the east end the rock is not quite so steep and the wall here might have been about 10 feet high. On the north side the wall was built a few feet higher. The average size of the stones on both faces of the wall is about 18 inches square by about 2 inches thick. In the centre the stones are of all shapes and sizes and some of them are round as if dug out of the ground. The wall is beautifully built but there is no trace of cement of any kind, earth or sand in it.

There were two approaches to the fort with entrances in the wall to correspond one on the north side, the other on the south side. The north approach is a steep gulley about 30 feet wide. About half way up there is a large stone which in the event of an attack could have been released and sent crashing down the gulley. The entrance through the wall could only have been about 4 feet wide. On the south side the approach commences at the foot of the hill and ascends zigzag fashion. About half way up there used to be a large heap of iron slag or cinder, and a large round hole faced with stone filled with ashes an charcoal which had evidently been used for smelting iron. At the top the track is so narrow that not more than three men could move abreast. A few yards to the west of the north entrance there is evidence of a well which had been about 3 feet deep by 6 feet in diameter. There is no sign of a spring and as this is the lowest point of the fort it may simply have been a collecting point for surface water. It does not appear to dry out except in very hot weather. In the north west corner close to the wall there is an enormous rock about 12 feet high by 14 feet square. Under the stone there is a cave about 12 feet long by 10 feet wide and 2 feet high. There is evidence that it must have been larger at one time.

There is no mention to be found anywhere that this was yet

another of Cluny's retreats, but almost certainly when Cluny was in hiding at Dalchully the Dun would have been a look-out post.

Cluny Castle rose from the ashes after Cumberland's butchery. It was replaced by an elegant country house of an Adam design. The connection with Cluny Castle ended sadly in 1943 and the historic contents were sold by auction. Some, however, were rescued by the then infant Clan Macpherson Association, and are now safely preserved in the Clan Museum at Newtonmore. When Queen Victoria stayed at Ardverikie in about 1850 she considered purchasing it as her Highland home but she was put off by the inclement weather in the district and bought Balmoral instead.

Cluny's Cage

THIS was an odyssey in the history of the Clan Macpherson, indeed in the history of the Highlands. Here Cluny's nine years of lurking in the heather ended. Much has been written of the Government's need for the capture of Cluny Macpherson, and the selfless devotion of his people. Browne in his book, *A History of the Highlands* writes more succinctly than others: Sir Hector Munro, then a Lieutenant in the 34th Regiment, was entrusted with the command of a large party, and continued for two whole years in Badenoch for the purpose of discovering Cluny's retreat. The unwearying diligence of the clan would alone have saved him from the vigilance of this party, directed as it was by an Officer equally remarkable for his zeal, and his knowledge of the country and the people. The slightest information, the slightest inattention, even a momentary want of caution, or presence of mind on the part of the Macphersons would have inevitably betrayed his retreat; yet so true were the clan, so strict in the observation of secrecy, and so dexterous in conveying to him unobserved the necessaries he required, that although the soldiers were animated by the hope of reward, and a step in promotion was promised to the officer who should apprehend him, not a trace of him could be discovered, nor an individual found base enough to give a hint to his detriment.

Many anecdotes have been related of the narrow escapes which he had in eluding the vigilance of the soldiers, especially when he ventured to spend a few hours convivially with his friends; and also of the diligence, alertness and presence of mind displayed by the people in concealing his retreat, and baffling the activity of his pursuers during a period of no less than nine years. At length, however, worn out with this dreary and hopeless existence, and taught to despair of pardon, he escaped to France in 1755, and died there the following year.

In *The Lyon in Mourning*, a collection of speeches, letters, journals, etc. relative to the affairs of Prince Charles Edward Stuart by the Rev Robert Forbes A.M., Bishop of Ross and Caithness, in three volumes (1746-1775), an account, in the handwriting of John Macpherson of Strathmashie, a close friend of Cluny, of the Prince's sojourn in Badenoch is given in Vol. III page 38. A portion of the narrative is given in Appendix 46 of Home's *History of the Rebellion* where it is stated that the letter was dictated by Cluny himself.

"After the catastrophe of Culloden on 16th April 1746, and the escape of Cameron of Lochiel, Cluny Macpherson and others, Lochiel, who was sorely wounded, came eventually home to Achnacary with a number of others, but on the approach of the Earl of Loudon with an army they had to disperse, and make for the Moor of Rannoch."

About the 20th June 1746 Cluny Macpherson, Macpherson of Breacachy and Sir Stewart Thriepland, physician, met him in a bothy on Ben Vrichk, and Sir Stewart attended his wounds. After a brief rest in the bothy, and Lochiel being somewhat recovered, Cluny led them thence for greater safety to Ben Alder. They were three months in hiding here before they learned that Prince Charles was safe and well at Achnacary. It was decided, however, that the Prince would be safer in their asylum on Ben Alder, and arrangements were made for Cluny to go to Achnacary on a certain day, and conduct him to Ben Alder. The impetuous Prince, hearing of the arrangement, was so eager to be with his two friends again that he set out for Badenoch immediately, fully expecting to meet Cluny on the way. But they missed each other. The Prince arrived in Badenoch on 29th August, and stayed overnight at Corineuir. Cluny who had gone all the way to Achnacary rejoined the Prince and Lochiel a few days later. Next day the Prince was led to Mellanmuir, a small bothy at the foot of Ben Alder where Lochiel, his personal ghillie, Alan

Cameron, Macpherson of Breacachy and two servants of Cluny were staying at the time. When Lochiel observed the approach of five men, the Prince, Lochgarry, Dr Cameron (Lochiel's brother), and two ghillies he instantly thought that they were from the enemy camp, which was not more than five miles from Mellanmuir. As he was in no condition to make for the hills he resolved that the "attackers" should be received with a general discharge of all their firearms, twelve firelocks and some pistols, but John Macpherson wrote: "as the auspicious hand of Almighty God and His Providence, which was so conspicuous in the escorting of his Royal Highness at all times prevented those within the hut from firing at the Prince with his four attendants they came so near at last that they were known by those within, and then Lochiel tho' lame made the best of his way to meet his Royal Highness without, who it may be believed received him very graciously".

The Prince appeared to be in good spirits despite the disasters, fatigues and difficulties he had undergone. The hut contained ample supplies of whisky, mutton, ham, butter and cheese laid in for Lochiel by Macpherson, younger laird of Breacachy. He drank copiously, and ate heartily of collops dressed with butter from a large saucepan which was the only utensil or crockery they had. There was only one refinement: the Prince ate from the pan with a silver spoon! At this point Cluny arrived back from Achnacary and joined in the repast. The next day Cluny decided to move further back into the mountain to a bothy called Uiskchilra, a poor, smoky habitation. Here he remained for two or three nights, and then removed to a very romantic, comical habitation made for him by Cluny two miles further into Ben Alder known as The Cage. It was a real curiosity, and almost defies description. "Twas situate on the face of a very rough, high rockie mountain called Letternilichk which is still a part of Ben Alder, full of great stones and crevices and some scattered wood interspersed. The habitation called the Cage in the face of that mountain was within a small, thick bush of wood. There were first some rows of trees laid down in order to level a floor for the habitation, and as the place was steep this raised the lower side to equall height with the other; and these trees in the way of jests or planks were entirely well levelled with earth and gravel. There betwixt the trees growing naturally on their own roots some stakes fixed in the ground, which with the trees were interwoven with ropes made of heath and birch twigs all to the top of the Cage, it being of a round or rather oval shape, and the whole thatched and covered over with foge. This whole fabrick hung as it were by a large tree, which reached from one end all along the roof to the other and which gave it the name of the Cage; and by chance there happen'd to be two stones at a small distance from one other in the side next the precipice resembling the pillars of a bosom chimney, and here was the fire placed. The smock had its vent out there all along a very stonny plat of rock, which and the smock were all together so much of a colour that any one coud make no difference in the clearest day, the smock and stones by and through which it pass'd being of such true and real resemblance. The Cage was no larger than to contain six or seven persons, from of which number were two frequently employed in playing at cards, one idle looking on, one becking and another firing bread and cooking."

Here Prince Charles remained for six days (September 6th to 12th) until news arrived by messenger at one am on 13th September that a French vessel had anchored at Loch nan Ualmh to transport him to France. He immediately set out on his last journey in the Highlands, and by daylight they had reached the old bothy of Uiskchilra. Here he was joined by his trusty aide de camp Col. John Roy Stewart of Kincardine for whom a search had previously been made. The reunion was joyful. That night the Prince, Lochiel, and their companions set out again and reached Corvoy by daylight on the 14th September. They continued their journey in the evening and went as far as Uisknifichit in the confines of Glenroy. Before it was daylight on the 15th they had reached the end of Glenroy, where they remained in hiding all day. By evening they were afoot again and reached the River Lochay in bright moonlight. Difficulties were encountered in crossing the river, but they eventually succeeded by crossing in relays in a leaky boat, and by midday they arrived at Achnacary where, because the enemy had burned and demolished every building, they were ill-off for any sort of accommodation. On the night of the 16th they were on the march again, and arrived at Glencamber at the head of Loch Arkaig where they were met by Dr Cameron and Cluny Macpherson who had prepared for the Prince's arrival with a plentiful supply of bannocks, and beef from a cow they had killed.

The parting of the ways came and Cluny Macpherson returned to his weary game of hide and seek with the enemy. On the 4th September, 1754, Cluny received a letter from Prince Charles in Paris commanding him to join him there as soon as possible, bringing with him all the effects he had left in his care, and whatever money he could lay his hands on "as he was at present in great straits."

In 1749, Dr Cameron, Lochiel's brother, had in his possession 6,000 *louis d'or* for which he gave Cluny his receipt. In a letter to the Prince dated 22nd June, 1750, Cameron of Lochgarry enclosed a statement from Cluny showing that about 16,000 might have been recovered, and suggesting that he and Dr Cameron should be authorised to bring it from Scotland. In spite of the terrible sufferings and hardships he had endured, and ever faithful to the Stewart cause, Cluny contrived to escape to France in June 1755, and in Paris duly accounted to the Prince for all the effects which had been left in his care. Cluny in his lonely exile and in ill-health as a result of his deprivations pined for the companionship of his wife who, after a long and perilous journey, joined him in 1757 and remained with him until his death at Dunkirk in February 1764 in his fifty-eighth year. He was buried in the garden of the house he occupied at the time. His sorely afflicted widow soon afterwards returned to Badenoch, and died in April, 1765. Her remains were buried in the Cluny burial ground.

Further information about Cluny's Cage is given in an old manuscript believed to have been written around 1756 which reads: "About five miles westwards of his (Cluny's) chateau commenc'd his forest of Ben Alder, plentifully stocked with dear, redhares, moor foul, and other game of all kinds, beside which it affords fine pasture for his numerous flocks and heards. There also he keeps a harras of some hundred mares, after which the fatal day of Culloden became the prey of his enemies. It was in this forest where the Prince found Cluny with Lochiell in his wounds, and other friends in his care. He (Cluny) was afraid that his (the Prince's) constitution might not suit with lying on the ground or in caves, so was solicitous to contrive for him a more comfortable habitation upon the south front of one of those mountains overlooking a beautiful lake of twelve miles long. He observed a thicket of hollywood; he went, viewed and found it fit for his purpose; he caused immediately wave the thicket around with boughs, made a first and second floor in it, and covered it with moss to defend the rain. The upper room served as salle a manger and bed chamber, while the lower served for a cave to contain liquors, and other necessaries. At the back part was a proper hearth for cook and baiker, and the face of the mountain had so much the colour and resemblance of smoke no person cou'd ever discover that there was either fire or habitation in the place. Round this lodge were placed their sentinels at proper stations, some nearer and some at greater distances, who day by day brought their notice of what happened in the country and even in the enemie's camp, bringing them likewise the necessary provisions, while a neighbouring fountain supplied the society with the rural refreshment of pure rock water."

This version generally agrees with John Macpherson's description and should be acceptable to the most ardent critic. Professor Walter Blaikie in his *Itinerary of Prince Charles Edward Stuart* says: "All traces of the shanty (an artificial structure of two storeys) have naturally disappeared but the site of the cave fulfills the necessary conditions, excepting that of the thicket of holly; yet, as trees have disappeared from many parts of the Highlands, the holly may have died out here." Presumably he was talking about the cave above Alder Bay.

The precise location of the Cage has been a matter of conjecture for many years. The spot marked on the Ordnance Survey map as Prince Charles' Cave, situated above Ben

Alder Cottage on Loch Ericht, is generally accepted as the site of the Cage, and it does to an extent fulfil some of the requirements of a hideout, but this belief is not shared by everyone: not by the author, and very decidedly not by John and Eileen Macpherson, Dalwhinnie. John was a stalker on Ben Alder with Eileen's father, Finlay Macintosh, that splendid Highland gentleman and notable stalker. Eileen lived there from 1920 until 1933 when her father became Overseer of Sir John Ramsden's eight estates, and they removed to Ardverikie. Eileen, now married to John, returned to Ben Alder in 1934 and they remained there until the outbreak of war in 1939.

They have an intimate knowledge of the ground and the history of the time. They also cannot accept that Cluny would have been so imprudent as to construct his refuge so near to Loch Ericht, the shores of which would no doubt have been regularly patrolled by Cumerland's troops, and the outlook from this point would have been severely restricted. The argument is irresistable.

After close study of the terrain the Macphersons are convinced that the Cage was sited by the Peregrine's Rock on west Ben Alder which is well up the Alder Burn, and high above it. From there the view to Corrour and the north west is uninterrupted. A lookout must have been posted south of there on the Doune, from which there is a clear view of the Loch Ericht valley eastwards to Binnein Mór to the north of Cluny Castle. From the Binnein the cave on Creag Dhubh could be signalled. All this appears to satisfy the requirements of John Macpherson's description of the Cage. Near the top of Ben Alder the ruins of three rough shelters may still be seen. Could they have been built by those sentinels about two hundred and forty years ago?

The estates of Cluny Macpherson were forfeited in 1765 but restored in 1784 when Cluny Castle was rebuilt by Duncan of The Kiln.

The Curse of Cluny

SOMEWHERE in the region of 1532 Cluny Macpherson gave his eldest daughter in marriage to one of the great chiefs of Ulster who came over from Ireland with a large retinue and warriors to celebrate the wedding festivities. One of the warriors Cathalan, or Catheolus, took full part in the honours being paid to his chief, but at the same time he found the time and means to court the bride's younger sister. They fell deeply in love, but, realising that Cluny would be unlikely to countenance a son-in-law who was not a chief in his own right, they decided to elope.

The time, however, was inopportune and Cathalan returned to Ireland with his Chief. In the autumn of the same year he returned to Badenoch with a faithful bodyguard, and soon made contact with the fair young maid of Cluny. Arrangements were made, and on the appointed day they fled to the wilds of the *Coire Dheirg* (Corryarrick) Pass aiming to reach the West coast and cross to Ireland by boat. Half way through the Pass the young lady became so fatigued that they sought shelter for the night in a small cave on a little hill which ever since has been known as *Creag a' Chathalan* (Cathalan's Rock).

In the meantime the alarm had been raised at Cluny Castle. The reason for his daughter's absence was reported to the old Chief. Summoning a body of the clan, he sent them in pursuit of the lovers, swearing that nothing but the Ulsterman's heart would satisfy his vengeance. In peril of their lives the clansmen must not return without it.

Meanwhile the lovers had left their refuge and were proceeding through the Pass. Snow had fallen during the night and blanketed the land. The pursuers traced their footprints and within two miles of the cave the lovers were overtaken. Cathalan fought fiercely, but was overpowered and murdered. After removing the heart, Cathalan's body was buried on the spot. The clansmen returned in triumph, with heart and errant maiden.

There is a sad ending to the tale. In Cathalan's wallet papers were discovered which proved him to be a person of high degree in Ulster. Old Cluny was filled with remorse for having caused his death, but in his pride he had it made widely known that it was no ordinary bonnet laird who had made so free with a daughter of Cluny Macpherson, and he erected a standing stone over Cathalan's grave. At the time it must have been a prominent landmark standing on a level space in the open glen. It is still there, but now much fragmented by years of erosion.

Strangely, nothing has been recorded about the young lady, but Cathalan's faithful bodyguard escaped by virtue of the fact that he had been sent ahead to arrange for a *birlinn* (barge) to carry the lovers to Ireland. He never returned to Badenoch to discover the fate of his Chief. Perhaps he guessed it, perhaps he had timely warning and wisely fled the country.

Oisean Macpherson

BALAVIL, just north of Kingussie, was the home of James Macpherson, popularly known as Oisean Macpherson. According to the *Old Statistical Account* the house stands on the site of the Castle of Raitts, but there is some confusion with the Castle of Rait in the Parish of Nairn. It is possible that this was the Castle to which the Comyns invited the MacIntoshes for their deadly feast. However, according to some historians the meeting was at the other Castle of Rait.

The house was built by James around 1790 and was originally called Belleville. It was designed by Adam as a country house. In 1903 is was burned and partially rebuilt. James' memorial is nearby, although he was buried in Westminster Abbey where he had been a parishioner.

James Macpherson claimed that he had given to the world the ancient songs of Ossian, or more correctly Oisean, the son and bard of Fionn the leader of the legendary Feinne. Controversy over their authenticity raged for years and continues to this day. Some claim them to be forgeries and James a charlatan. Be that as it may they at least brought Celtic literature to the notice of scholars all over Europe, and drew attention to the immense value of ancient Gaelic manuscripts which were in grave danger of being lost for all time.

The following significant passage is extracted from *Voyage Round the Coasts of Scotland and the Isles* by James Wilson:

> In the district of Steinscholl a man died about twelve years ago named John Nicolson or MacCormaic, at the very advanced age of 105. There is one circumstance connected with this old man's history worthy of notice, which is, that he could repeat the most

of Ossian's Fingal Temora &c with great fluency, and precision. The writer of this heard him say that he committed these beautiful poems to memory, from hearing them repeated when a boy by his grandfather. If this fact be not sufficient to establish the authenticity of these unparalleled poems, it must surely establish the truth that they existed before the time of Macpherson who attempted to translate them into the English language. The silly allegation that Ossian's poems were Macpherson's own production is palpably confuted by MacCormaic and others who could repeat them before Macpherson was born.

The Cave of Raitts

THE cave which was at one time called *An Uamh Mhór* (the Big Cave or the Robber's Cave), is now generally known as the Cave of Raitts. It is situated on a ridge to the west of the A9 above Lynchat, a mile or so north of Kingussie. In the vicinity of the cave the ruins of an ancient settlement are to be found.

The name Raitts, according to one authority comes from the Gaelic word *Ràt* or *Ràth*, meaning a place set apart for Druidical rites, or for the purpose of religious worship. To this day glebe lands are sometimes called *Rath Mhinisteir*, the Minister's land or portion. *Rath*, without emphasis on the vowel, may also mean prosperity or profit. Another authority claims that *rath* is an old Irish Gaelic word meaning a dwelling inside a hill, and this would appear to be apt in this particular case.

In 1835 the cave was examined by Sir David Brewster, the distinguished philosopher, who was a guest of the Macphersons of Balavil. It was filled with stones and rubbish, but on clearing out all the debris he was astonished to find a long, subterranean building, faced on each side with stone, and roofed by a gradual constriction of the sides which were then joined with large flagstones. Shaped like a horseshoe, its convex side faced south, and the entrance was at the centre of this side by means of two stone steps, and a passage of some length. To the left was a separate compartment with a door. An unusual type of lock, almost all eaten up with rust, was found in the debris.

Sir David averred that there was no tradition about the history of the cave, and as far as he knew it had not previously been noticed. He could not have made much enquiry locally, because the Rev. William Blair, a Minister of Kingussie from 1724 to 1786, referred to it in his diary. Even then it was falling in, and "you could see only a dark hole through which you could not see the far end." The roofing flagstones, he noted, were about twelve feet long. It was seventy feet long, eight feet wide and seven feet high.

"Old Biallid" (Captain Lachlan Macpherson of Biallid) who died in 1858, aged 89, wrote an account of it prior to 1835. He referred to it as the MacNiven's Cave, and that at that time it was almost intact.

It is described in *Castellated Architecture of Scotland* by David MacGibbon and others. "It curved as shown on the plan. The side walls were built with large stones, those towards the top being pushed inwards so as to diminish the space, and the top covered in with a long stone as shown in section. The entrance is very narrow, and has apparently sloped down from the surface to the door which is composed of massive stones, the jambs of which incline inwards towards the top. This doorway has been defended either by a stone or wooden door, strengthened by a strong sliding bar on the inside, the holes or slots for which are still visible. The portion of the roof next the entrance has fallen in, but the greater part of the stone roof still exists."

It seems certain that the *Uamh Mhór* was an ancient earth or Erd House as it is typically Celtic in architecture, for no other earth houses outside the area of Celtic influence in Britain, Europe or the world have the peculiar curvature as shown in the drawing. The architecture appears to be that of Scotland's Iron Age, the pagan period of the Celtic people.

The granite slabs roofing the cave may well be the "Standing Stanys de Rathe de Kyngucy", a ring which was perhaps the biggest and most important stone circle in Badenoch. The circle is recorded as a Mote or Judgement Place, where the Wolf of Badenoch held court in 1380 for the Bishop of Moray to show his titles of land tenure. The Bishop, however, disagreed with the Wolf's authority, and refused to stand inside the circle. Outside the circle was unofficial ground where an oath was not necessarily binding.

A tradition claims that it was built by a giant race in one night. The giantesses dug it out, and carried the spoil down to the Spey. In the meantime the giants were quarrying the stones, and building the cave.

The first known inhabitants of the cave were the MacNivens, hence "Old Biallid's" reference to it as the MacNiven's Cave.

There is, however, a more interesting legend attached to Raitts. In the distant past part of Badenoch was in the possession of the MacNivens, who were vassals of the Comyn, Earl of Badenoch. When the Macphersons lost their patrimony in Lochaber they found asylum in Badenoch. It was only after some years, when Robert the Bruce drove out the Comyns, that the Chief of the Macphersons was able to purchase the lands of Cluny. This so alarmed the MacNivens that they lost no opportunity in insulting Cluny Macpherson, who was so outnumbered by the MacNivens that the insults had to be accepted with as much dignity as the Macphersons could muster. The breaking point was inevitable, and when MacNiven, who then resided at Breakachy in Laggan, poinded Cluny's cattle, Cluny again decided on diplomacy. He sent his daughter to treat with MacNiven, but instead of receiving the courtesy due her rank and sex, she was insulted and treated in an unchivalrous manner. Her petticoats were removed and she was sent home to her family along with the poinded cattle. The bull's tongue had been cut out, and this was regarded as a direct challenge. This was too much for Cluny, but a direct conflict was out of question in view of the superior number of MacNivens.

One of the Macphersons, called *Alasdair Cainnteach* (Loquacious Alexander) gathered round him a hundred resolute men. They set out in the dead of night, and by sunrise the next morning only eighteen MacNiven men remained alive. The survivors hid themselves in the woods around Raitts, and successfully evaded the vengeance of Alasdair Cainnteach. In stealth they were able to excavate and construct a cave under the farmhouse floor of Raitts, and here with skill and secrecy they dwelt during daylight hours for several years.

Alasdair Cainnteach had suspicions about the farmhouse, and decided on a stratagem. He concealed himself from public view until he grew a long flowing beard, then in the guise of a beggar he came to the farmhouse late one evening. He was kindly received by the women, but lodgings for the night were firmly refused. He begged to be allowed to stay, but they were adamant. When they attempted to remove him forcibly he pretended to be afflicted with "gravel" (concretions in the kidneys or bladder), and uttered such piercing shrieks that they took pity on him, allowing him to lie in front of the fire, where he pretended to fall asleep. Believing him to be dead to the world the women opened a trapdoor in the floor, and handed down food to waiting hands. This was observed by Alasdair and the next morning he left the house early. He returned in a few days with a strong party, and beheaded all the MacNivens on a tree stump at the door. It is a strange coincidence that to this day, all the descendants of Alasdair Cainnteach are said to suffer from the malady of gravel.

East of the cave stood the castle of Raitts, the dungeons of which are now the cellars of Balavil House. The Castle was the scene of a famous banquet held by the Comyns. At this time they were Lords of Badenoch, but were becoming increasingly aware of the rising power of the Macintoshes.

In previous encounters the Macintoshes had shown their mettle. The Comyns thought it was wise to sue for peace, and invited the Macintoshes to a feast as a gesture of goodwill. The Macintosh Chief knew only too well the old couplet deriding the Comyn's good faith:

Cho fad 's bhios craobh 'san choille
Bidh foill na Chuimeaneach —

(As long as there will be a tree in the wood
The Cummings will be deceitful) —

and having been forewarned of treachery, had alerted his bodyguard who were seated alternatively with their hosts. At a concerted signal each Comyn was to stab his neighbour to death. The given signal was a boar's head on a wooden platter, but the Macintoshes were so much on the alert that the tables were turned, and at the first sight of the platter each Comyn suddenly felt cold steel in his belly.

N.B. The restoration and preservation of the *Uamh Mhór* has been discussed in various quarters recently and hopefully some action will be taken in due course.

Big Farquhar,
The Invertromie Giant

AT THE time of the Red Comyn, Invertromie was farmed by Big Farquhar, a giant of a man, reputed to be over eight feet tall. He was a man of peace, except when roused to defend himself or his property. Then he was a terror. Despising the sword, he armed himself with a stout oak cudgel, and was reputed to be able to ward off as many as ten assailants.

He lived happily with his wife Màiri, for many years and they had a son. On reaching manhood the son left Invertromie and joined a band of freebooters from Lochaber. Then domestic troubles arose when Farquhar and his wife quarrelled. She left him to live with *Domhnall Dubh* (Black Donald), a forester who had a strongly fortified home in Glentromie, and nine sons. Big Farquhar found it irksome living alone, and soon created a clash of tongues when it became known that he was wooing a lady of the Baron's court. Their clandestine meetings had been going on for some time, when finally the lady agreed to quit the castle and live with Farquhar. They were observed by a retainer leaving Ruthven Castle and it was reported to the Baron who ordered that the pair should be brought back.

"How dare you, varmint, take away Mistress Grace without our leave", thundered the Baron.

Cunningly Farquhar replied, "The lady wished to see her nest before chosing her mate, and if it pleased her, my Lord, we were to crave your permission."

"Was that so wench? Speak", shouted the Baron. "If it please my Lord I am willing to go with him now", Mistress Grace replied humbly.

Addressing Farquhar, the Baron said, "You will have the

64

choice of two ways to end the matter. You will either be tied in matrimony at St. Columba's, or by the hangman's rope at Ruthven."

Such was the Red Comyn's arbitrary way of settling affairs, giving no thought about the bigamous nature of the marriage. Naturally the marriage was solemnized in St. Columba's, and Farquhar and Grace appeared to be blissfully happy. Farquhar even gained favour at the Castle through the good offices of Grace's brother, the Baron's chief henchman. Occasionally Farquhar's roving, reiving son paid a flying visit, and it was said that on such occasions beeves found their way to the folds of Invertromie as well.

There was an amicable arrangement between the giant and his real wife. They visited each other occasionally, but showed no desire to live together again. She appeared to be quite content to keep house for Black Donald, while Grace held the affections of Farquhar.

A time came when Farquhar's flocks began to dwindle mysteriously. A watch was kept, and a gang was seen driving away some lambs. There was a scuffle and one of Farquhar's servants was killed. Farquhar was so enraged that when the gang returned to his henhouse a few nights later he rushed out, laying about them with his club to such good effect that he killed three before the rest took flight. There was consternation when it was discovered that one of the dead was a Petty Officer and the others Privates in the Baron's bodyguard. A council was held at the Castle to consider the best way of securing the Baron's vengeance. Finally a party set out to arrest Farquhar, but he had been pre-warned by a message from Grace's brother, and he planned to flee north to Grant country and wait until the Baron's anger had cooled. Instead he went to Black Donald's house for succour. In addition to being a stronghold with secret escape doors, it also formed no mean garrison when manned by Black Donald, the nine sons and Farquhar himself. Farquhar remained in seclusion for a month before venturing out of doors. He created a huge armchair in the face of a rock overlooking the main entrance to the glen, and here he came and sat every day to spy the glen track. The chair became known as *"A'Chathair Fearchar"* (Farquhar's chair). A travelling pedlar, whom he knew and trusted, visited secretly and gave him all the news.

Time wore on, and Farquhar became fat and lazy under the care of his wife whose administrations began to fester so much in Black Donald's mind that he was goaded into hatching a scheme to kill Farquhar. After discussing the matter with his sons it was decided that Black Donald would shoot Farquhar as he drowsed in his chair. The sons were to be close at hand in case they were required. Farquhar was shot with an arrow through the heart, and died without a groan. His body was dragged to a nearby burn which they diverted. A deep channel was dug and the body buried in the channel, obliterating all traces of the crime.

They returned home with the story that Farquhar was seized by a hunting party and taken to Ruthven. Unfortunately for Black Donald the pedlar was approaching the chair with news for Farquhar and observed something amiss. He watched carefully, and saw the whole foul deed. Retracing his footsteps he sought out Farquhar's son, who was in the forest, and informed him of his father's death. Early next morning Black Donald and his whole household were aroused by the barking of dogs, and battering at the doors. Black Donald peeped out, and saw Farquhar's son with a party. He demanded to know their business.

Farquhar's son replied, "You have murdered my father, your guest. Come out and fight for I mean to make a cairn of your heads on yonder *creag* (hillock)."

Black Donald replied with a shower of arrows. Màiri, at a lower loophole saw and heard everything, and spying the pedlar she beckoned to him. From him she heard the whole story; whereupon she unbarred a secret door and admitted a number of the invading party. Black Donald's men were taken unawares, and they were slain to a man. Their heads were cut off, and piled on top of a knoll that stands near the glen road between the farmhouse of Killiehuntly and Glentromie Shooting Lodge. To this day it is called *Tom na Cheann* (Knoll of the Heads).

Farquhar's son gathered all the stock and goods he could find, and, taking his mother with him, escaped into his retreat in Lochaber.

The massive rock called Farquhar's Chair is easily found just below the old ruined kennels East of Glentromie Lodge. It is naturally padded with moss, and makes a comfortable seat. Probably it is natural, and Farquhar had no hand in shaping it.

The Black Officer

CAPTAIN John Macpherson, popularly known as *An t-Othaichear Dubh Baile A'Chrodhain* (The Black Officer of Balachroan) was born at Glentruim in Badenoch in 1724. He was the second son of Alexander Macpherson of Phoineas, an ancient cadet branch of the Macphersons of Invereshie. His mother was a MacDonald of Aberarder, and in true Highland fashion it was said of him that the best blood of Badenoch and Lochaber ran in his veins. From both families sprang many distinguished officers of the British Army.

Iain Dubh MacAlasdair (Black John, son of Alexander, as he was known in his younger days), was no exception, although he was well on in years when he obtained a commission. Not a great deal is known of his military exploits, but it is believed that he distinguished himself in a number of engagements. He was the Recruiting Officer in Badenoch for a number of years. It was in some respects a disagreeable post, always highly unpopular, and one which carried many occupational hazards; but so assiduous and successful was he that of the number of recruits from the superabundant population no fewer than seventy became commissioned officers. It was claimed that his methods of recruitment were not entirely ethical, and he earned a black reputation among the people. The tales about him grew, and with each telling they became embellished and more exaggerated, as is the way.

It was said that he attended every market, ball and gathering in the district, and mingled freely with the young men, treating them liberally to as much whisky as they could consume. When they became insensible, he would press a shilling into their hands, and declare them enlisted in the

King's Army. In the case of the more wary, who declined to drink beyond a certain point, he would slip a shilling into their glass or pocket, and with dire threats claim them as willing recruits. He would even follow a young man on the road and surreptitiously slip the dreaded shilling in his pocket, or if the man were approaching him he would throw the shilling towards him. If he was unwary enough to catch it he soon found himself sent off to the wars.

One Sunday on his way to Church he caught up with the stalwart young cleric who was to preach that day.

"Ah", said the Captain to himself, "you are too fine a figure for black clothes, red would suit you better, and if I am any judge a red coat will be on your back before long."

They entered the Church together, but the Captain's mind was too preoccupied with recruiting matters to be diverted by the preacher's eloquence. The young man was the only son of a poor widow who lived in a distant part of the Strath. At ten o'clock the next morning the Black Captain was hammering at the widow's door. He was courteously invited in, but no sooner was he seated than he abruptly came to the point of his errand. The widow was immediately thrown into a state of terror, and implored the Captain to have compassion for her. The response to her entreaties was, "It is a pity to see such a good looking young man dressed in black", and without another word Black John threw a shilling into the preacher's lap. The next day he was marched away to Edinburgh.

It is little wonder that the loved ones of those who were so tyrannically impressed into the army heaped the blackest of curses on the Captain's head, and invoked Heaven's direst vengeance to fall upon him, and prayed that the Devil himself would carry him off to a place of torment.

When he retired from the Army, Captain Macpherson became tacksman of the farm of Balachroan, where, after marrying late in life, he settled with his wife and children. He had one son, Colonel Gillios Macpherson, and two daughters. Balachroan, the ruins of which still exist, stands on a ridge above the old A9 between Kingussie and Newtonmore. It was built in the old baronial style with whinstone and granite, and slated with grey stone from a local quarry. Macpherson became totally engrossed in agricultural pursuits and hunting. As an agriculturist he was ahead of his time. He introduced new methods of farming, and better types of grain and root crops which resulted in crops superior to any others in the district. His cattle were fatter and sleeker, and produced rich milk in quantities previously unknown in the district. His methods were so far in advance of the primitive husbandry of the time that they gave rise to much speculation in the Spey Valley, and in Badenoch especially. This added fresh fuel to the conviction already held that he was *"deisciobul an Diabhol,* (a disciple of the Devil).

Weird tales began to circulate about shrieks and groans emanating from the cellars of Balachroan, and at many a fireside the old people spoke in hushed tones of his compact with the Devil, and how he had at his peril even outwitted the Prince of Darkness. In the course of their relationship, the Devil had promised to give him, for a certain period of time and on certain conditions, all that he might desire. First, the Captain asked that all the crops at Balachroan should be the wonder and envy of those who saw or heard of them. The Devil readily agreed, providing that he would get the roots. That year the fields at Balachroan carried nothing but grain, and the harvest the Captain reaped was almost beyond belief. In due course the Devil arrived to claim his share, and the Captain coolly told him to take the roots according to their agreement. The Devil was furious and accused the Captain of cheating.

"All right then" the Captain replied, "I will give you the crop next year and keep the roots for myself."

With astonishing lack of guile *Donald Dubh* agreed. The following year every field at Balachroan carried root crops, potatoes, turnips, carrots. At harvesting time Satan arrived and demanded his share. Pointing mockingly to the shaws the Captain said, "There it is as agreed. Take it."

Blacker than ever and fuming with rage the Devil howled, "You will not cheat me a third time", but the wily Captain did.

70

His next wish was to be given a herd of cattle the like of which was never before dreamed of in the Highlands, and Old Nick agreed, providing that all the beasts in the corner nearest the steading would be his share. The Captain immediately put his plan to cheat his master for a third time into operation, and after demolishing the whole steading built a circular one in its place. Soon it was stocked with the finest cattle in the length and breadth of all Scotland, and when the Devil called to collect his dues, and was told to claim all that he could, according the their agreement, he positively screamed with frustration when he could see no corner in the steading.

If John Macpherson was as evil as he was reputed to have been, and if he had outwitted his master as the people claimed, then assuredly retribution was approaching nearer, and nearer by the hour. There are different versions of how he met his untimely death, but the one which gains most credence in Badenoch is that recorded by the Rev. Thomas Sinton in his book *The Poetry of Badenoch*. It was given by a resident of the district who knew the Black Officer and all the members of the party who perished along with him. He also had a first hand account from members of the search party who found the bodies in a tragedy which became known as *Call Ghaidhig (The Loss or Catastrophe of Gaick)*. A memorial stone stands at the scene of the tragedy.

At this time Captain Macpherson was tenant of Gaick Forest, and frequently went there on hunting expeditions. He stayed in a bothy on the east side of the glen, just behind where Gaick Lodge now stands. It was a sturdy stone building roofed with sods of heather and strongly reinforced below the foundations. The previous year the Captain had arranged with some friends to meet at the Post Ban's house, the croft of Aultlearic between Newtonmore and Kingussie, to prepare for a big hunt at Gaick on Christmas Day 1798. None of his friends appeared, however, at the appointed time and the Captain was in a black rage. When the Post Ban suggested that the hunt should be postponed until the next day the Captain shouted violently, "No, I made an appointment and I must be in Gaick tonight." Fearfully the Post Ban agreed to

71

accompany him. Taking guns, two dogs and some food with them the set off up Glen Tromie and arrived at the bothy just before midnight. There they lit a fire and made supper. All the time the Captain was restless and irritable, and drank copiously from his flask.

Suddenly the dogs began to growl and bare their teeth. They were tied up, and the Captain ordered the Post Ban to go to bed. In a state of unease the Post Ban lay down on a heather bed and wrapped himself in his plaid, but could not sleep.

Meanwhile the Captain continued to pace restlessly up and down muttering to himself, and repeatedly drinking from his flask. Finally there was a knock at the door, causing the dogs to growl loudly and strain at their leashes. The Post Ban sprang from his bed, but was ordered to lie down. "Stay where you are, I will go", and when he opened the door the Post Ban glimpsed a tall dark figure before the Captain closed it behind him.

Fully alert, and trembling with fear the Post Ban strained listening to the voices raised in altercation. One voice sounded like a billygoat, and all he was able to make out was the Captain promising that he would be there again in a year's time, and he would assuredly be accompanied by a party of men.

When he re-entered the bothy the Captain was white and trembling. After another long pull at the flask he said shortly, "It was just a gentleman I had invited to the hunt, but he was so annoyed by the lack of company he decided to go home."

"Has he far to go?" asked the Post Ban.

"Quite a long way", replied the Captain, "but he has a fleet horse."

The next day the Post Ban carefully examined the ground when the Captain was otherwise engaged, but not a trace of a single hoof print could he find. On his return home the Post Ban related to his wife and closest friends all that had transpired at Gaick, and the news soon spread round the district. Now the people knew that the Black Officer was in league with Satan, and he was shunned, and held in greater dread than ever.

It was also recalled that a month before the tragedy, when Captain Macpherson was staying in the bothy, some of his companions observed what appeared to be a fire on top of the hill above the bothy. Filled with curiosity to see a fire in such an unlikely place they climbed the hill to investigate, but when they reached the summit no trace of fire was to be found. Here, surely, was an ill omen.

As another Christmas approached it became known that the Captain was trying to arrange another hunt at Gaick; but on one pretext or another all who were invited declined the invitation. No one risked causing offence by a direct refusal. However, on Monday 30th December 1799, four men with dogs and guns did assemble at the Post Ban's house and set out for Gaick. Despite the entreaties of his parents, Iain Ban, the Post's young son, was determined to join in the hunt. Another eight men, who had either been cajoled or threatened by the Captain, arrived but they did not leave Aultlearic for some hours after the Captain and his party.

Now that very morning young Iain had acquired a new pair of brogues for the occasion, but as the second party approached Nuidebeg the uppers mysteriously parted from the soles of the shoes, and he was left barefoot and unable to continue. His companions were immediately overcome with superstitious fears. As they recalled all that Iain's father had told them about his experiences of the previous year, they saw a portent in this unusual occurrence, and decided to return with Iain. Meanwhile the Black Officer and his party had reached the bothy at Gaick, but they were never seen alive again. When they set out for Gaick the intention of the Black Officer had been to return the following Friday bringing home a supply of venison for a Christmas feast on Monday 6th January 1800. As he was about to depart from Balachroan an old, faithful servant, Belle Campbell, took off one of her garters and with it fastened his plaid more closely about his shoulders, little thinking that in a few days time she would be helping to lay out his remains.

It had been settled weather for some days, calm and frosty, but on Wednesday evening, 2nd January 1800, a terrific storm

73

blew up and many people narrowly escaped with their lives. It continued with unabated fury until the afternoon of Friday 4th January, when it blew itself out leaving the air clear and cold. The whole district was covered with a deep blanket of snow. The hunting party did not return as expected that night, and the next morning a messenger set off for Gaick to discover the fate of the party. When he arrived at Linn nam Biorag, a crofting community occupied by Stewarts who had originally come from Atholl, he learned that a terrible catastrophe had occurred. The bothy and its occupants lay under an avalanche of snow.

In Badenoch, speculation was rife and some strange, ancient, methods were used to discover the fate of the hunting party. The popular method for obtaining information was to seat upright on a *cogan* (a wooden utensil) the youngest member of a family, and question the child. This was resorted to in a house at Nuide the day after the storm. "Will they return tonight?" the child was asked. "No." "Will they return tomorrow?" "No." "When will they return?" "Never, never", answered the child.

When the messenger returned in haste from Linn nam Biorag, on Sunday, a group of men set out from the Church at Kingussie the next day for the scene of the disaster. With the help of the people from Linn nam Biorag they made considerable progress in clearing the snow, which lay to a depth of several feet. Daylight began to fail, however, and they had to return home in defeat.

They returned the next day, Wednesday, with reinforcements led by an old soldier. It was calm and fair, and when at last the area was cleared of snow they found that the bothy had been completely demolished. The dead bodies of the party were discovered thus; Balachroan lying in bed on his face, James Grant and John MacPhail also in bed with arms stretched over each other. Donald MacGillivray was in a sitting position with one hand down at his foot as if in the act of taking off his shoes. Duncan MacFarlane's body was found two months later by a fox hunter about three hundred yards from the bothy. It was lying in a wreath of snow one hand pointing upwards.

The assumption was that he had perhaps been upright when the avalanche struck the bothy, and had been carried away with the wreck of the building of which only the foundation stones were left; whereas the others on their heather bed on the floor were protected by the base of the wall. The debris was carried for a distance of three to four hundred yards, and part of the roof for nearly a mile. The guns were twisted in all shapes, mangled by the stones and timber of the building for it was constructed in a substantial manner with walls of heavy stone four feet high. The area in the centre was divided by a strong partition. All this weighty mass brought down with such violence would satisfactorily account for the state of the guns.

The bodies were placed in the rough deal coffins which the party had taken with them, and, with the remains of the Black Officer leading the mournful procession, they started to make their way down the Glen. Before they had gone a mile or two they were beset by another violent storm of wind and snow, and had to seek shelter. The wind was so fierce, and the snow so blinding that further progress seemed impossible. In this dilemma the old soldier is reported to have said *"Cuir an diabhol sean air a chuil"* (Put the old Devil in the rear), and to their amazement the storm abated as quickly as it had arisen, and they were able to resume their journey without further incident. To avoid the deep snow in the bottom of the Glen they held to the ridges as much as possible and, descending by Allt Ghiuthaish and Balintian of Nuide, they forded the Spey below Balachroan.

The destruction of the bothy was not the only catastrophe of that terrible night; part of a sheep fank and a poind fold near Loch an t-Seilich, about two miles distant, were also swept away. From the south side of Loch Ericht an immense body of earth and trees had been carried across the ice to the north shore where it was to be seen for many years after, at least a quarter of a mile distant from the place it was torn.

The Black Officer was laid to rest in St. Columba's Churchyard, Kingussie, where, for seven hundred years, generations of Macphersons have been laid. The flatstones over the grave bears the inscription "Sacred to the Memory of Captain John Macpherson, Balachroan, late of the 82nd Regiment, who died 2nd January 1800, aged 76 years."

A contemporary scribe recorded that ". . . the Glen in snowstorms is subject to terrific avalanches by which the deer sometimes suffer; and upon one occasion a herd of ten stags and hinds was suddenly overwhelmed in sight of a celebrated deer hunter and gentleman of the Strath who was stalking them at the moment when the rolling volume of snow descended the mountain and buried them in its bosom. Some years afterwards, by an awful catastrophe of the same kind, when on a hunting expedition in the Glen he himself, the party by whom he was attended and several fine deerhounds, and the house in which they lodged were swept away . . ."

Gàidhig dhubh nam feadan fiar (Dark Gaick of the twisted ravines) — if Gaick had ever been notoriously demon haunted it became even more so now. Here at *Leum na Feinne* (the Leap of the Feinne) the wild and profligate Walter Comyn had been torn limb from limb by two infuriated witches in the form of eagles. Here a deluded hunter, sheltering in his bothy when mist and darkness encompassed the hills, met a similar fate at the hands of his unearthly paramour, and much later *Muireach MacIain* (Murdoch son of Iain), another noted Macpherson hunter who married a daughter of Macpherson of Phoineas, met the notorious Witch of Laggan. It was said that a single hair from her head could sheer like cheese the strongest oak beam.

Little wonder then that a place so much associated in the people's minds with such tales should not at once relate the startling events described, and ascribe them to more than natural causes.

It was discussed in every hamlet in Badenoch, Strathspey, Lochaber and Strathdearn, and with each recital it became more exaggerated. It was a judgement, the people cried, and the calumnious verses of a rhymster, Donald MacKay, were continuously reprinted and widely distributed. It grey into a supernatural romance by virtue of the imagery in the minds of the people. It was said by some that the bothy had been torn apart in a vortex of thunder and lightning, launched by vengeance of Heaven against sinners; by others it was attributed to a whirlwind raised by the Devil for the same chastisement; the detention of those who were prevented from accompanying the lost party was ascribed as dreams, warnings, and other supernatural interposition to save them from the wrath to come. Fertile imaginations, a natural love of the marvellous, and lapse of time accomplished the rest, until the minds of the populace there was no greater bogle in the Central Highlands than *An t-Othaichear Dubh Baile a'Chrodhain*.

Whatever the Black Officer's faults and failings as a recruiting officer, another side to his character must be recorded. Even if he had been able, or inclined to set aside all laws divine or human, he was still under the observation of his fellow countrymen, and amenable to their opinions. Among his contemporaries were many fine gentlemen of honour and justice who would not have brooked injustice to the most humble of their clansmen. There is not a single instance on record of his ever having forfeited their regard for him. On the contrary, the celebrated Mrs. Grant of Laggan, whose *Letters from the Mountains* are famed in and far beyond the Highlands, wrote about him with warmth. The respective families were on friendly and intimate terms, and "Mr. Grant (her revered husband) was always partial to him."

A contemporary was James Macpherson of Ossian fame for whom he negotiated the purchase of several lairdships in the district, among them the ancient patrimony of Phoineas the Captain's own home.

Another contemporary was Malcolm MacIntyre, a bard whose genius was less recognised than many who were much less gifted. Often he attended the Captain in the chase over a long period of intimate friendship, and after his death wrote a moving elegy which is unsurpassed in the Gaelic language. It wells from the bard's sorrowing heart and extends to fifteen stanzas. The tender prelude reads:

'S beag ioghnadh mi bhi dubhach
Air feasgar 's a 'ghrian le bruthach
Bheir mulad air suilean sruthadh

'S i 'n Molluig so thionndaidh chairt — dubh oirnn

(It is not a wonder that I should be mournful
Evening will bring the sun down literally with the brave
Sorrow will cause eyes to flow
'Tis this yule that has turned a black card for us)

Another eloquent tribute to the Captain's memory was penned by his clansman, Captain Lachlan Macpherson of Biallid of lasting memory. "Old Biallid" was conversant with all the details, current opinions, traditions and actual occurrences in which the Black Officer figured. He wrote of him in glowing terms in *Lays of the Deer Forest* by the Sobieski Stuarts which was published by Blackwood in 1848. He bore testimony to Captain Macpherson's qualities as a perfect Highland gentleman with few equals. "He was kind", he eulogised, "generous, brave and charitable; a friend of the poor and needy, and none who sought his aid went away empty handed."

At the instigation of Mr. James Macpherson of the Union Bank, Edinburgh, a memorial stone was erected on the site of the bothy in the year 1902 and inscribed with the names of Captain John Macpherson and his companions, Donald MacGillivray, John Macpherson, Duncan MacFarlane and Donald Grant.

Donnachadh Gobha (Duncan MacKay), another contemporary bard also wrote an elegy on the loss of Gaick and under the names of the above men the last stanza was inscribed in Gaelic:

O duisgibh-se mu'm fas sibh liath,
'S dluithibh bhur cas ris an t-sliabh,
Feuch gu'm bi bhur fasgadh deant
Mu'n teid a'ghrian a laidhe oirbhe

(Oh, waken before you go grey
Quicken your foot towards the moor
See that your shelter is made
Ere the sun sets on you).

As a result of weathering the inscription on the stone is now unreadable but thanks to the interest and generosity of the proprietors of Gaick Forest a stainless steel plaque bearing the full inscription has now been bolted to the foot of the stone.

The Ruthven Ferry

BEFORE a bridge was built across the Spey the only way of crossing from Ruthven to the Kingussie side, or vice versa, was either to ford the river, which could be hazardous, or cross by the ferryboat at a charge of one penny. The boathouse was on the Kingussie side and stood in a hollow to the east of the present bridge. The ferryman was, of course, a person of some consequence in the community, but at the time of this tale the encumbent was an unprincipled, surly character.

The Spey was big in spate when Communion Sunday arrived, and taking advantage of the situation the rascally ferryman raised the fare to sixpence. The result was that a number of people who had come a long distance to celebrate the sacrament were both unwilling and unable to meet such exertion. Included in the number was a pious old lady who had come a long way for fifty years to attend Communion. After pleading with the ferryman for some time, even promising to pay at a later date, she was refused the crossing and had to return home. Her absence we commented upon by the Minister and elders who feared that illness had caused her non-attendance. A few days later an elder paid her a visit, and found the poor old soul very ill in bed. In the course of conversation the elder learned with horror the reason for her absence. On his return to Kingussie he went straight to the boatman's house, and confronted the ferryman.

"You cruelly refused to bring a poor woman across the river so that she could attend the sacrament of our Lord because she had not enough money to satisfy your greedy soul", he thundered. "For this vengeance will overtake you here and in the hereafter. You will be deprived of your living, your house and your land, and be sure of this you will die an unnatural death, and your body will be devoured by beasts."

It is remarkable how this prediction was fulfilled. About a year later a bridge was erected over the Spey, and the ferry fell into disuse. The ferryman moved to the village where he earned a bare living at odd jobs.

At the time a meal mill stood somewhere near the centre of Kingussie High Street, and here the ferryman occasionally found work. One day he was sent to close the mill sluice which meant he had to walk a narrow plank from the mill loft to the sluice. He turned the water off, but he did not return to the mill. Observing after some time that the ferryman was still absent the miller went to investigate, and hearing a commotion amongst the pigs he turned his attention to the pigsty. To his horror he discovered the ferryman's body being devoured by the voracious beasts. In all probability the ferryman had slipped off the narrow plank into the pigsty immediately below, and so frightened the pigs that they attacked and killed him.

Red Murdoch of Ruthven

EVEN before Saint Columba founded his Chapel at Kingussie Ruthven was a thriving, populous little clachan nestling around a castle which was said to have existed from time immemorial. It was no sooner destroyed by the ravages of warring tribes than another was built on its ruins. It was only in the shadow of such strongholds that the people felt safe to continue their daily rounds of work and play. But their safety was secure only as long as they remained loyal to the lord and master of the castle who had the power of life and death over them, dispensing rude justice as his pleasure or policy dictated. No one dared to dispute or question his orders. Sometimes the seneschal, who was employed to see that his orders were carried out, was more of a tyrant than his master, and against such monsters the people frequently plotted.

In the time of Red Murdoch the lordship of Badenoch was vested in one of the Comyns, or Cummings. He was reputed to be a son of the Red Comyn who was first designated as Lord of Badenoch. By tradition he was as infamous as his father, and exceeded both his father and his descendant, the notorious Wolf of Badenoch, in the degree of his despotism and debauchery. His seneschal was Red Murdoch whose excesses were even worse that the others: a petty tyrant, an oppressor of the people, a pitiless abettor of his Lord's wishes, and a relentless fiend when pursuing his own whims. Old and young dreaded the sight of him, and avoided him like the plague.

On a fine morning towards the end of August he was seen approaching the Clachan with armed guard and trumpeters. When they arrived at the centre of the village the trumpeters blew a loud blast, and in a thunderous voice Murdoch announced in his Lord's name that in three days every able-bodied female between the ages of twelve and thirty would have to appear stark naked to sheer the Baron's corn.

The people were confounded, and could hardly believe that such unprecedented cruelty could be brought upon them by another human being, but knowing the lustful nature of the Baron they realised that clemency could not be expected. It was impossible for them to flee the neighbourhood, and in any case if anyone did succeed in escaping, retribution would be brought on his kindred.

But all was not lost. One beautiful young girl had reason to dread the approaching day more than the others because she was aware that by his leering glances Red Murdoch had singled her out as his own particular prey. She confided in her sweetheart whose grandmother was reputed to be a witch, and he comforted her with these words, "Have no fears; neither the Baron nor Red Murdoch will live to see the day."

And so it transpired. The Baron was soon after in Atholl, and on a certain day it was arranged that he would ride back over the hills with the close companions who accompanied him to Atholl. Red Murdoch with a bodyguard was to meet him half way. On the morning before that appointed for the women to sheer the corn, Red Murdoch mounted and left Ruthven with a bodyguard of two men to meet his lord and master as arranged. But they were never seen alive again. At dusk a horse cantered up to the gates of Ruthven bearing in the saddle part of the mangled trunk and legs of the Baron.

At dawn a search party set off into the hills, and in a narrow valley at Gaick they found fragments of clothes and flesh adhering to human bones which clearly indicated that a fearful battle had been fought, and the Baron and his evil companions had at last received their just deserts. No one, especially the women, mourned their loss. The site of the struggle became known as the *Bealach nan Chuimeanach* (Pass of the Comyns).

The Bewitched Mill of Banchor

THE Old Mill of Banchor above Newtonmore, the ruins of which can still be seen in a crook of the River Calder above the Farm of Biallid, had a weird, almost supernatural history.

It was a busy mill for it supplied the countryside with all the meal it required, but on one day every year, the 12th of February, it remained idle. This was known as *Latha Feile Breidh* (St. Bride's Fair Day), on the eve of which the miller turned off the lade and locked the mill door. Neither he nor any member of his family would dare to go near the mill until the day had passed, nor would the locals go near it. They were so careful in the observation of the custom that they left not a straw, not an ear of corn, not a speck of meal belonging to them inside its walls. The origin of the custom is obscure, but the most popular belief is as follows.

In remote times a widow with two children had a croft in Glen Banchor, not far from the mill, and paid for her rent in kind. However, hard times came upon her and she fell in arrears. Threatened with eviction she sent all her corn to the mill for grinding, but the miller was a rogue and abused her trust in him. He informed another creditor who promptly seized the corn and carried it away. The poor woman and her children were in due course evicted on a cold wintry day, and made their way towards Lochan Ovie under Craig Dubh where a small clachan existed. In one of the houses lived the woman's grandmother who was reputed to be a witch. On the way the party was overtaken by a fierce snowstorm and perished. When the grandmother was told about the tragedy she promptly invoked a curse on both the miller and the creditor. Soon after corn was brought to the mill by the creditor, and after it had been put in the kiln to dry they both retired to bed. The next morning, alerted by smoke rising from the mill, neighbours discovered the kiln burned to the ground, and the charred bodies of both men lying together with a broken bottle between them.

The event was a topic of conversation for long after, but opinion was divided, some believing that the bottle was more the cause of the fire than the old witch's curse.

The miller's brother took over and rebuilt the kiln. Within a year he had lost a hand in the machinery, and soon after he became so ill that he died. Then the whole establishment was destroyed by fire. The mill was such an absolute necessity to the community that it was forthwith rebuilt. Public feeling was so aroused by these unaccountable calamities that attention became concentrated on the witch and a deputation approached the old woman and begged her to lift the curse. Witches cannot subsist on air any more than us and she partly relented, but still upheld the curse to the extent that anyone working in the mill on the anniversary of her daughter's death would suffer terrible consequences.

For generations *Latha Feile Breidh* was religiously observed by succeeding millers, then it fell vacant once again and a certain miller was persuaded to run it for a year on trial. He was a man of property, and attached little importance to the supernatural. He announced that he would break the spell by working on the prohibited day. Warnings from friends and neighbours fell on deaf ears. When *Latha Feile Breidh* arrived no one had corn in the mill, and the miller was left to his own devices. He did have some corn of his own for milling, but no sooner had he started up the mill than he detected a curious grating sound which was beyond even his practised ear. But he continued until the grinding was finished then he commenced to sieve the meal. To his chagrin and amazement, he found it was mixed with grit and sand, and quite useless as food for man or beast.

When he examined the grinding stones he found the bottom one cracked in three places. Having arrived at the conclusion that it was an accident he decided nevertheless to hide the broken stone, destroy the meal, and keep the matter to himself. A new stone from another mill secretly replaced the broken stone, and he let it be known that despite the curse the mill worked perfectly on the forbidden day. The confidence of the people was restored and orders poured in, but the miller's troubles were not at an end. Despite all his confidence he could not get the mill started, and all his art and skills were of no avail. A millwright was called in but in vain. Then horror! The granary was found to be swarming with rats, and the whole store of grain was reduced to a few husks. The miller was so disgusted that he gave up the mill before the year of trial had expired, and returned to his own mill. But misfortune followed him; his mill went on fire, his stock sickened and died, his property melted to nothing, and he died a comparatively poor man.

In time another tenant was found; a God-fearing, honourable, charitable man who was highly respected by all. Some years before, he had adopted an orphan gypsy boy, and the two of them ran the mill successfully for a number of years without a single hitch, but always giving due observance to "the day". When the old man died and another miller took over the tenancy the mill once more began to give trouble. In desperation the miller sent for the gypsy lad and asked him if he would start it. "Yes, of course", he said, "providing you leave me alone at it." Undetected he took a small piece of wood from a secret hiding place and entered the mill alone. In a matter of minutes the mill was in motion again.

The boy was pressed to reveal the secret of his success, but this he scornfully refused to do. It now became clear that the mill could not be run withut him and he became the miller, although with little success. People began to complain about poor quality meal and bad measures. Custom dwindled to nothing, the gypsy disappeared, and the mill fell into a state of decay. Thereafter the unfortunate crofters of Newtonmore and Strone had to cart their grain to the mill at Kingussie.

The Three Wishes
and Black Donald

JOHN MACNIVEN was a crofter from the Braes of Ruthven. His wife *Meg Mhor*, or Big Meg, was a stout muscular woman. They were a thriving, happy couple except for one thing: they had two daughters but no son, and they bemoaned their lack of an heir.

Near the house was a small, tree clad fairy knoll and often the fairies could be seen playing and dancing in the moonlight. In a small stream nearby they washed their gossamery clothes. Meg knew that if she could catch one of the fairies she would obtain her dearest desire, so she fell into the habit of keeping a careful watch on the burn, and one fine dry morning she spied one of the fairies busy washing her clothes. The fairy did not observe Meg's stealthy approach, and as the fairy's powers of becoming invisible lay solely in being fully clothed Meg had little difficulty in catching the little creature.

"Let me go, let me go", pleaded the fairy, "and I shall grant you any three wishes you choose."

"Give me sons", cried Meg, "make me a good spinner; grant that our cows may be good milkers, and carry quey calves."

"Granted", said the fairy, "all are granted", and picking up her garments she immediately disappeared.

In the course of time Meg bore seven fine sons; she became an expert spinner, and the cows became noted for their good quality milk. Invariably they produced quey calves. The sons became famous athletes, and were so fleet of foot that they could outrun a hare as easily as a greyhound. They in turn produced sons who became equally famous in the district.

The last of the lineage in Badenoch was *Domhnall Dubh*

(Black Donald). For a time he served in the Black Watch, but deserted and returned to Badenoch. Word was sent to Captain John Macpherson, the local recruiting officer, to arrest him if possible and send him under escort to Inverness.

As a result of his customary vigilance the Black Captain, or *Othaichear Dubh* as he was known locally, eventually captured Donald at Newtonmore, and putting handcuffs on him they set out for the prison in Kingussie. On the way the wily Donald appeared to become very penitent. He praised the Army, and solemnly recommended his guards to enlist. So pleased was Captain Macpherson with his prisoner's change of heart that when they reached the Inn of Aultlearic, he called a halt and ordered a dram for them all. Donald's handcuffs were removed so that he could have his dram also, and watching for the opportunity he suddenly bolted across the meadow, plunged through the Spey and made for the wilds of Gaick.

The Black Officer was in a towering rage and offered a tempting reward for the recapture of Donald. In the meantime Donald lived the best way he could in Gaick Forest, but a week or so after his escape Donald sought *fasgadh 's cairdeas* (shelter and kindness) at Nappach, the home of an old friend called Peter MacDuff. He was warmly welcomed and provided with a dram and a good supper. Then Peter showed him to a comfortable bed in the barn, wished Donald a good night's rest, and locked the door behind him. Donald was no simpleton. Suspecting that Peter's extra kindness was motivated by rather more than friendship he contrived to escape from the barn, and hid himself in the heather.

Within the hour Captain Macpherson with a few local men, who assisted him in carrying out his duties, arrived on the scene and surrounded the barn. The door was unlocked but to the Captain's chagrin, and Peter's, the bird had flown. Livid, the Captain vented his spleen on Peter. Just then Donald coughed.

"*Eisd*" (listen) said the Captain "I heard him cough." Recklessly Donald shouted "You heard me, but you can't see me; if you saw me you couldn't find me; if you found me you couldn't catch me, and if you caught me you couldn't hold me", and with a loud laugh he leaped up and raced across the moor. He was never again seen in Badenoch.

The Forester of the Fairy Corrie

IN St. Columba's Church, Kingussie, lies, it is believed, the dust of the forester of the Fairy Corrie who was a native of Cowal in Argyll. He was of the MacLeod's of Raasay, and being very fair his descendants were called *Clann Mhic-ille Bhain* (Children of the fair, or literally white-haired man, who now call themselves White or Whyte). It was universally believed that the forester had a *leannan-sith* (fairy sweetheart) who followed him wherever he went. The late Duncan Whyte of Glasgow was one of the eighth generation in direct descent from the forester, and he had a fund of stories about his famous ancestor. Perhaps the most interesting concerns his death and burial, and the sad fate of his *leannan-sith*.

In 1644 when the Earl of Argyll was in pursuit of Montrose from Aberdeen through Banff, Moray and Strathspey, the forester was in Argyll's Army, and his fairy sweetheart, in the form of a white hind, followed in the wake of the Army. While they were in camp near Ruthven Castle, opposite Kingussie on the East side of the Spey, some of Argyll's Officers started to mock him about his camp follower. Argyll was a touchy man and wrathfully he commanded some of his soldiers to shoot the hind, but despite aiming accurately not a single bullet pierced her. It was noted that the forester disobeyed the command, although his gun was loaded and aimed. He was brought before Argyll who commanded that he alone should fire at the hind. Quietly and with dignity he said, "I will fire at your command Argyll, but it will be the last shot I shall ever fire." And so it happened. Scarcely was the gun discharged when he fell dead on the spot. As for the fairy, she gave an unearthly scream and disappeared in a cloud over the shoulder of a hill.

James Macpherson, The Reiver

AS THE result of an affair with a beautiful gypsy girl in the 17th century Duncan Macpherson of Invereshie fathered a son of whom he was inordinately proud, openly acknowledged, and brought up in his own household. As the boy grew he became increasingly strong and handsome, but on account of his heritage proud, impulsive and wreckless, and a swordsman of note. His two-handed claymore was six feet long, and broad as a scythe in the blade; his much scored targe was of wood, covered with hide and studded with brass nails. Both were preserved by the Macphersons for long years after his death.

When he had just reached early manhood his father was killed in a clan affray, and young James became a roaring, ranting freebooter; gay and witty, and the life and soul of any gathering he attended, always ready and willing to play a reel on his violin for he was, in addition to his other attributes, a remarkably fine fiddler and rhymester.

His attitude to life was similar to so many of his contemporaries, to wit that the only respectable occupation for a *duine uasal* (Highland Gentleman) was to plunder, not only the neighbours with whom he was at enmity, but the countryside at large. And yet he had a streak of nobility in his nature. It was said that no cruelty or atrocities attended any of his forays, and if he plundered the affluent he gave generously to the poor. He was a man of iron will, but he had one weakness in his armour, he could neither resist a pretty face nor could any girl resist his charm. This was to lead to his first arrest for freebooting.

His forays frequently took his as far as Aberdeenshire, and the authorities became assiduous in their efforts to capture and sentence him. But at every turn he evaded the snares laid until they recalled his weakness for women, and taking advantage of his vanity they bribed a pretty girl to lure him into a chosen rendezvous on the pretext of listening to his exquisite violin music. Guilelessly he walked into the trap and was seized by the Law Officers. Realising that she herself had been duped the poor girl was filled with remorse, and immediately started to consider ways and means of setting Macpherson free. She knew that Peter Brown, a notorious freebooter and chief of a tribe of gypsies, had close ties with James and would be only too happy to connive at his friend's escape from jail. Brown straight away gathered his tribe, and sent word to Badenoch begging Donald Macpherson, James' cousin, to come and help in the rescue.

When all arrangements had been made the rescue party secretly entered Aberdeen, and converged on the jail. A stall was erected in front of the prison door, conveniently hiding it from view, and Brown and Macpherson set to work forcing an entrance. They soon found James, but he was securely chained to the wall of his cell. Anticipating this Brown had come prepared with the necessary tools, and set about cutting James free while Donald kept guard at the door. Many of the people who had gathered at the prison knew full well what was afoot, but having great regard for James they crowded round the jail entrance to thwart any attempt by the Law Officers to prevent James's escape. But one man in the crowd, a local butcher, knowing that a reward would be given if the attempt to free James was foiled, climbed on top of the stall and leaping on top of Donald threw him to the ground. Donald grappled with him and the two rolled about on the ground, hammering and tearing at each other in such frenzy that their clothes were torn off. The butcher's strength suddenly began to waiver and in desperation he called his dog, but Donald grabbed his own plaid and wrapped it round the butcher. Misled by the scent, the dog attacked his master and tore his thighs so badly that the butcher was no longer fit to continue the fight.

Meanwhile Peter had succeeded in freeing James and the

three fugitives took to their heels and fled. The Law Officers had stretched webbing across the Gallowgate to prevent their escape, but Donald quickly hacked it to ribbons with his sword. The three speedily made their way to a pre-arranged rendezvous where horses were ready waiting for them. Soon James and Donald were galloping towards Badenoch.

It was inevitable, however, that James's wreckless exploits would lead to his eventual undoing. Two things contributed to his downfall; his love of women and his gypsy blood. He joined forces with Peter Brown, and fell in love with one of the tribe. His infatuation with the girl, and his arrogance and confidence made him careless. This was all carefully observed by the Banffshire lairds who were sorely tried by the escapades of James and his boon companions, Peter Brown, Donald Brown and James Gordon.

They bided their time, and finally, one day in the year 1700, the three became involved in a pointless brawl at a market in Keith. The brawl soon became a riot, and the three were captured and fettered by command of James' oldest and worst enemy, Duff of Braco. They were held under close guard, and brought quickly to trial. They were indicted by the Procurator Fiscal — "Being knoune habit and reputed to be Egyptians and vagabonds, and keeping ye mercats in ye ordinaire manner of thieving and purse-cutting, or guilty of the rest of the crimes of theft, and masterful bangstree and oppression."

When the accused appeared in Banff Court the Laird of Grant protested in the strongest terms against the proceedings. He claimed that as they lived within the regality of Grant, over which he had "jurisdiction of pit and gallows", they should be tried by him. Nicholas Dunbar of Castlefield, who was Sheriff of Banff, over ruled him, and instructed that a jury should be empanelled for the following day. Despite the fact that the evidence was more concerned with their evil reputations than sound fact they were all found guilty, and with unseemly haste the Sheriff ordered that James Macpherson and James Gordon should be removed to the tolbooth, and from thence in eight days time to be led to the gallows, and there to be hanged by the neck until dead.

The Sheriff and his associates, in particular Duff of Braco, were more determined to rid the country of at least James Macpherson than to abide by the strict tenets of the law, for the unusual short period between sentence and execution seemed to argue that they feared some intervention. An intervention, albeit unavailing, there certainly was. Not only was public sympathy with James, but powerful influences were being exerted on his behalf.

On the day appointed for his execution it became known to the Banff Law Officers that a reprieve was on its way by special messenger. But Dunbar arranged for the messenger to be intercepted and delayed outside the town, while the time of the execution was brought forward by a few hours. Nothing would be allowed to stand in the way of the execution, and when James was led to the gallows, holding himself with nobility and pride, it was noticed that he carried his famous fiddle with him. In a strong voice he told the crowd gathered at the gallows that while in prison he had composed a song which would be his epistle. Then talking the fiddle under his chin he sang his epitaph, 'Macphersons farewell':

> My father was a gentleman
> Of fame and lineage high,
> Oh!, Mother would you ne'er had borne
> A wretch so doomed to die.
> But dantonly and wantonly
> And rantonly I'll go
> I'll play a tune and dance it roun'
> Below the gallows tree
>
> The Laird o' Gat with power aboun
> The royal majesty,
> He pled full well for Peter Brown
> But let Macpherson die.
> But dantonly and wantonly
> And rantonly I'll go
> I'll play a tune and dance it roun'
> Below the gallows tree
>
> But Braco Duff in rage enough
> He first laid hands on me.

If death did not arrest my course
Avenged I should be
But dantonly and wantonly
And rantonly I'll go
I'll play a tune and dance it roun'
Below the gallows tree

I've led a life o' meikle strife
Sweet peace ne'er smiled on me,
It grieves me sore that I must go
An' no avenged be.
But dantonly and wantonly
And rantonly I'll go
I'll play a tune and dance it roun'
Below the gallows tree.

When he had finished James held up his fiddle and asked if anyone in the crowd would accept it as a gift, on condition that they would play the same tune on it at his wake. But the people were so cowed by the presence of so many of his bitter enemies that none dared to accept the offer. So with a laugh James smashed the fiddle across his knee, remarking that as it had often been a great comfort to him it was fitting that it should perish with him, and with these last words he was launched into eternity.

Donald, his cousin, who had been effacing himself in the crowd, managed to retrieve the neck of the fiddle and bring it back to Badenoch where it was preserved by Cluny Macpherson. The remains of the famous fiddle are preserved to this day in the Clan Macpherson Museum at Newtonmore.

James Gordon was also hanged that day and this was the last case of execution by hanging in Scotland under the old heritable jurisdiction. The Browns were jailed, but after a year they broke jail and disappeared quietly into the countryside. In the early years of the 19th century James's grave was opened, and revealed his enormous frame which confirmed the tradition that he was exceptionally tall and strong. His exploits continued to be recounted over ceilidh fires for many years, but his lasting memorial is the song he played on the gallows hill at Banff in the year 1700.

Loch a' Bhrodain of Glen Tromie

ONCE upon a time Calum Ban, a hunter, lived in a cottage near Loch a' Bhrodain, the name of which is supposed to derive from Brodain, a hound or mastiff. Calum was a notable hunter, but he was known chiefly for his influence on dogs. One night he was awakened by a scraping noise on his door, and when he opened it he was confronted by a demon holding a litter of fine pups in his arms. He told Calum that for a number of reasons he would not be able to rear them himself, and begged Calum to do this service for him. He would, he said, return for them before they were fully grown and Calum could keep one for himself. Calum agreed, and the demon disappeared into the air. The pups were lovingly nurtured, and grew into the finest gun dogs Calum had ever seen.

At the time there was a story that a beautiful white hind roamed the corries of Ben Alder. She was a fairy hind, claimed by some to be Greinne herself, the wife of Fionn. She was so fleet that no living dog, it was believed, could overtake her, but Calum thought that with such dogs as these anything was possible. Unfortunately, when he was about to commence their training the demon returned to collect his pups. He was about to carry them off when Calum reminded him of his promise. In a rage the demon seized the smallest pup and, breaking one of its hind legs, threw it at Calum exclaiming that such a mortal as he must never think that he could have a dog to vie with his. Calum was furious, but kept silent and as soon as the demon had gone he bathed the broken leg with leaves he knew had healing properties, and splinted it with small willow branches in such a way that the poor animal could not put any weight on it.

In a surprisingly short time the leg healed, and the dog became as fast as lightning on the hill, but it always ran dot and carry one. Now the training of Brodain, as Calum named the dog, commenced and the pair were inseparable. In the course of time they were hunting in the vicinity of Loch Ericht when they spied the white fairy hind. Calum sent Brodain in pursuit, but swift as he was he was no match for the fairy hind. She fled swiftly in the direction of Gaick, but as she approached the loch she appeared to be tiring and Brodain began to gain on her. Like a flash she sped to the loch and plunged into it with Brodain at her flank, and neither of them were ever seen again.

The Green Fairy Dogs

IT WAS near the old castle of Ruthven that the last of the fairy dogs was seen, and this, according to tradition, was only about one hundred and seventy years ago. Green fairy dogs were not considered particularly malevolent, except for one terrifying fact. It was said that if one followed you, and barked within your hearing three times, it was a death omen unless you had the courage to turn and stone it at the first bark.

A story is told of an old shepherd's encounter with one of the green dogs. He lived alone, except for his dog, in a remote cottage far up in the hills, and one evening as he sat by the fire making a shepherd's crook he heard scratching. Thinking it was his dog returned from driving the sheep from a cornfield close by, he rose and opened the door. Only the wind entered. "Come in at once", he cried, "I will not be holding the door open all night for you", and what should enter but a green dog with golden eyes and crimson ears which went to lie by the fire. The old man sat down in consternation and picked up the crook, but it was not of the crook he was thinking. What should he do? A fairy dog was a chancy companion in a lonely cottage at night, and the shepherd felt ill at ease. He had after all invited the dog in, unwittingly perhaps, but the dog was in a sense his guest and had to be treated accordingly. It seemed cold and tired and never once barked. The shepherd rose and placed food and water near the great hound. It drank greedily of the water, but left the food untouched. Then the shepherd's own dog scratched for admittance, and when it was let in and saw the creature by the fire it flattened itself in terror. The green dog raised its head and made a strange sound in its throat but nothing resembling a bark, and moved a little aside to let the shepherd's dog near the fire. Whereupon, all terror gone, but guardedly it came to the fire, ate its supper and lay down under its master'schair. So they sat throughout the night, and when dawn broke the green dog rose, shook itself and walked to the door. The shepherd made haste to open it, but on the point of departure a very strange thing happened. The dog put out its tongue, pink and soft as a rose petal, and licked the hand of the astonished shepherd.

Summer and the autumn passed and winter came upon the hills. One bitter day of ice and snow the shepherd's dog got his paw crushed while following his master down an icy slope. The shepherd carried him home, and washed the damaged paw carefully before applying a poultice of dry birch leaves. That night it snowed hard, and at dawn the shepherd set out to gather his sheep, leaving the willing but useless dog behind. All that day he worked hard finding and digging out sheep, but he was handicapped without his dog. He was an old man, and his exertions began to sap his strength.

"If I leave the sheep they will die; if I die my dog will die", he muttered as he struggled bravely on.

Suddenly there was a flurry of snow driven by an icy gust of wind, and out of it emerged the green dog. "Aye", thought the old man, "this is it now", and too exhausted to run he braced himself for the bark which never came. The big hound approached him, and gently licked his hand again with his soft, pink tongue. Miraculously vigour and warmth flooded the shepherd's veins, and he drew himself erect. The dog threw back its head and bayed, and the moor was instantly alive with fiery-eyed green dogs.

Backwards and forwards they quartered the ground gathering the sheep, and when one found sheep buried it waited, pointing until the shepherd came and dug out the stranded animal. Then he was led to a small, sheltered corrie free of snow, and there he found all his sheep grazing contentedly with green dogs on guard. Soon the great hound who had been his guest nudged him towards the cottage, and when they reached the door the pink tongue again caressed his hand. The shepherd bent to pat his friend's head but there was nothing there but empty air.

The Fairy Dogs of Loch Gynack

THERE was always some doubt about the existence of fairy dogs. One body of opinion averred that they were simply fairies, while another held firmly that there were actually fairy dogs, but the fairies were so dissatisfied with the breed that they were always trying to obtain well bred earth dogs for crossing purposes, in the hope that their own breed would thus be improved. There is reason to lend support to the second view as we shall see.

A crofter and his family who lived near the loch were in a bad way; nothing he could do improved matters, and his children continually cried out with hunger. Thinking that if he disappeared someone would take pity on his wife and children he decided to drown himself, and with this in mind he made his way to the loch. So that all might know he was dead he took off his coat and boots, and as he advanced to the water he saw before him a beautiful woman of friendly mien. She greeted him kindly, and soon he was confiding in her all his troubles.

"Foolish man", she said, "go home to your wife and children and all will be well if you will only agree to one condition."

Impulsively he cried out, "Any condition."
you tonight when you reach home."
"Every wish you have will be fulfilled if you promise to meet me a year from today and give me whatever, or whoever meets you tonight when you reach home".

Quickly recalling that his last sheep had died a few days before, and the orphaned lamb tethered near the door would surely be the first thing to greet him, he readily agreed and made his way home with a joyful heart. But his wife had seen him coming, and with the children at her heels ran out to greet him. But his dog outstripped them and jumping up licked his face.

A year passed and the crofter, now reasonably prosperous and comfortable at last, felt he could not part with his faithful dog. He confided in his wife and she indignantly said, "We owe every bit as much to her work as to the fairies. Oh, Calum, you must offer everything you have to save her." Calum, his dog at heel, made for Loch Gynack with a leaden heart, and there he found the fairy waiting for him. The poor dog growled in fear. Calum explained to the fairy how they felt about the dog, and offered instead all his stock as ransom for the dog. But all his entreaties were of no avail. The fairy insisted that she have the dog and nothing else.

Stubbornly Calum said, "I will not give you the dog; take back all your gifts."

"That includes you life Calum; but for me you would now be dead."

Then a strange thing happened. The dog left him, and crawling on its belly in fear went to the fairy. The fairy spoke to it in a soft crooning voice and the dog rose, licked his hand and returned to the fairy's side.

"Meet me here a year from today, Calum", said the fairy, and along with the dog disappeared into the air.

A year to the very day found Calum on the shores of Loch Gynack again. And again the fairy was waiting to greet him, and with her Calum's old dog and a most beautiful pup. The dog bounded to him, leaping up joyfully and licking his face.

The fairy smiled and said, "She's mine, Calum, the best dog in all the world, and only once more will you ever see her. When your time comes she will come to you and warn you. The puppy is yours, take it and go home."

So Calum thoughtfully returned home, the puppy to heel. Calum trained it as only he could. It became the best working dog in the district, and its descendants had fairy dog characteristics in that they all had silver eyes and could see the wind.

Now Calum had become an old man, and one day when he went to the hills he met once more his old dog. Prophetically it barked three times and Calum knew that he had only three more days to live. He said goodbye to his old friend and companion and patted its head. It licked his hand and Calum turned homewards to set his affairs in order.

The Devil at Loch Gynack

THE Devil was reputed to haunt Loch Gynack, and spend some months there every year. When he emerged from the loch in Spring he was said to have created such a wave that the nests of the *stuirteags* (black-headed gulls) close to the water were flooded. This provided the devil with much merriment because these gulls are said to be messengers of the angels, and have within them the spirits of the people who were filled with good deeds while on earth, and so qualified to be angels themselves. Meanwhile they expiate whatever sins they may have been guilty of by wearing the distinguishing black cap on their heads.

His Satanic Majesty is supposed to have taken up residence near Kingussie because Kingussie was forgotten when Sodom and Gomorrah were destroyed. It was said that people who were too wicked to live in Kingussie took up residence in Newtonmore. And certainly there lived in Newtonmore at that time a rascal who claimed that he could make new and better eyes out of lead. Scenting him out as one of his own the Devil came to call, and so persuasive was the rascal that he prevailed upon the Devil himself to be fitted with a pair of eyes made from red hot lead. In this way the rascal claimed to be responsible for the death of the Devil but, of course, no-one, however simple, believed him for a moment.

The Watch Hill of
the Black Watch

AFTER the Black Watch Regiment was raised in the early part of the last century, around 1893, detachments of the Regiment policed various parts of the Highlands in an effort to suppress cattle thieving, a common practice at the time, for the people lived largely by the principle:

> Because the good old rule
> sufficed them, the simple plan
> that they should take who have the power,
> and they should keep who can

Because of its strategical position in the Monadh Liath range on the west side of the Spey Valley, the summit of the hill which became known as *Carn an Fhreiceadan* (The Watch Hill), although of lesser altitude than the surrounding tops, was chosen as one of the principle stations from which to observe movements in the valley below. From the summit on a clear day a wide view can be obtained ranging from Ben Nevis to Skye, north to Sutherland and Caithness, and east to the hills of Banff and Aberdeenshire, so that no matter from which direction the reivers were returning they were under observation from *Carn an Fhreiceadan*. When the alarm was given by smoke signals suitable measures were taken to spring on the marauders and relieve them of their booty which was in due course returned to the rightful owners. Unfortunately, the regimental records at Balhousie Castle, Perth, shed little or no light on the period. The Companies under John, Earl of Atholl, were raised "to watch upon the Braes where thieves and broken men doe resort, within the Shires of Inverness, Nairn, Moray, Bamff, Aberdeen, Mearns, Angus, Perth,

Clackmannan and Monteith, Stirling and Dumbarton.

The strongholds appointed for the incarceration of offenders included Inverness and Nairn, the Castle of Ruthven of Badenoch, Murray and Bamff—Balachaisteal in Strathspey."

Even the early records of the Regiment, as embodied at Aberfeldy (May 1740), were lost at sea off the Irish coast round about 1768, and again off the coast of Flanders in 1793. A glimpse of these marauding days appeared in the August 1847 edition of the *Inverness Courier*. It came from the memories of *William Ban Macpherson* (Fair William Macpherson), who died in 1777 at the age of 100. When he was a boy of twelve herding cattle near Dalwhinnie, he witnessed, on a fine autumn day in 1689, a herd of lifted cattle being driven westwards along the banks of Loch Ericht by a fierce-looking band of Lochaber reivers.

He had the temerity to accost the men, and ask where they had come from. He learned that the cattle had been lifted in Aberdeenshire, and that the reivers had reached this far without challenge. They proceeded on their way and halted for the night at Dalunchart, which is now called Ardverikie, feeling secure now that they were within a day's march of home. But only a few hours after they had left, a body of fifty well-armed horsemen appeared, leading horses laden with bags of meal and other provisions. They were led by a courteous gentleman who beckoned William to approach. The boy was closely questioned about the movements of the reivers, their numbers and equipment and William Ban, curious to see what would transpired followed in the wake of the horsemen.

Towards dusk they drew near the encampment of the thieves who were busy roasting one of the bullocks over a roaring fire. A council of war was held by the horsemen, and the leader anxious to avoid spilling blood unnecessarily suggested a flag of truce with the offer of a bag of meal and a pair of *brogans* (shoes) for each man. Believing the proposal to be a sign of cowardice on the part of the horsemen the offer was scornfully rejected, whereupon at a signal from their leader the horsemen attacked, and soon all but three of the reivers escaped unhurt and fled westwards to tell of the sad end of their companions.

Not all cattle reivers, however, were without redeeming qualities. A notable reiver was *John Dubh Cameron* (Black John). He was a man of massive physique who had been out in the '45 and on this account he was called Sergeant Mor, but that is another tale.

The Sergeant Mór

JOHN DUBH CAMERON, who was called the Sergeant Mór (big sergeant) on account of his powerful figure recruited, a band of reivers after the '45 Rebellion and levied blackmail in Rannoch, Badenoch, Lochaber and Mar.

On one occasion he met a Redcoat officer who had lost his way in the wilds of Laggan. He confided in Donald that he was carrying a large sum of money for the garrison at Fort William and felt apprehensive about encountering the Sergeant Mór. He requested Donald to accompany him on the way and as they walked they talked much of the Sergeant Mór and his deeds. The Redcoat unwisely referred to him as a robber and vile murderer. "Stop," cried Donald, "he certainly takes booty from the Whigs and the Sassenachs, but neither he nor his companions have ever shed innocent blood except once when unfortunately a man was killed at Mar. I immediately ordered the *creach* to be abandoned and returned to the owners."

"You?" said the Redcoat. "What concern was it of yours?"

"I am John Dubh Cameron", replied John, "I am the Sergeant Mór. There is your road to Inverlochy. You and your money are safe, but tell your Governor to send a more wary messenger for his gold in future. Tell him also that although I am an outlaw by force of circumstances I am a soldier like himself and would never stoop to rob a defenceless man who confided in me." The Redcoat hastily departed for Inverlochy but he never forgot his adventure at Laggan and frequently related the story.

King Nechtan

DUNACHTON HOUSE has a venerable appearance, but in fact it is not an old building having been built on the site of a former residence of the Macintoshes which was destroyed by fire in 1869. The dungeons of the old manor were utilised until 1956 when Colonel Prior, who had bought the Estate from the Macintosh of Macintosh in 1937, died. The Estate was purchased by a nephew, Sir Andrew Forbes Leith of Fyvie Castle.

To the West of the house there is a hillock called *Tom a' Mhòid* (The Court of Justice Knoll) where the Lairds of old dispensed justice in their own summary ways. Behind Tom a' Mhoid another hill is called *Creag Righ Tharoild* after King Harold, giving some credence to the belief of Viking presence in the district. There is a tradition that a force of Viking raiders was defeated in the vicinity by Nechtan, King of the Picts. Dunachton is derived from Dun, a castle or fort, and Nechtan the Pictish King who was, by all accounts, a great warrior king in his younger days.

When he was well past his prime, and his prowess in the use of arms was diminished, his agility of mind had, it seems, by no means deserted him. A Pretender to the throne forced him to abdicate, but before the newcomer had time to settle in a second Pretender appeared on the scene with a strong force. The usurper gathered his forces and went out to meet the challenger. The ensuing battle was fierce and bloody, and the challenger was slain. There were dire losses on both sides.

In the meantime Nechtan, who was fully informed of the course of the battle, ascended the throne, and when the usurper returned to Dunachton, Nechtan, with a much stronger force behind him, dared him to usurp a second time. The Pretender retired licking his wounds, and Nechtan was left in peace to complete his reign, no doubt well pleased with his own astuteness.

Below Dunachton House are the remains of St. Drostan's Chapel, *Capella de Nachtan* built around 1380. It is believed that Drostan was an early Pictish Saint before the time of Columba. The Chapel stood within the ancient walled burial ground situated in the Chapel Park below the ruined castle.

There is an ivy clad building in the cemetery and on each side of the doorway an inscription. On the right hand side the inscription commemorates Captain George Macintosh of the Sixtieth Regiment who died in 1780. On the left side we are told that the tomb was erected by his wish and expense. He may have been a brother of William Macintosh of Balnespick who was tacksman of Dunachton at the time. The tomb is in the form of a Chapel with a large window in the east gable. The Barony of Dunachton was at one time held by the MacNivens. The last of the line were two heiresses one of whom, Isobel, married William Macintosh a cousin of the Chief, and himself later, Chief of Clan Chattan.

The Green Gown of Alvie

IN bygone days there lived a farmer at Alvie called Duncan Macintosh. Duncan himself was a tall and exceedingly handsome man, but his wife Betsy and their seven daughters were far from being prepossessing. Betsy was, however, a capable housewife and mother, and for a time they were happy in their home and family. But Betsy began to suspect that Duncan's affections had strayed elsewhere for he had become moody and morose, and frequently wandered the hills far into the night, neglecting both family and work. Squabbles ensued, and they led cat and dog lives.

Betsy commenced to keep a guarded watch on Duncan's every move. She noticed that regularly every evening about eight o'clock he set off up the glen behind the farm, and she determined to discover the purpose of his visits. One evening she followed stealthily at his heels, and in fury observed a beautiful young lady dressed in a green gown join Duncan at a small rounded knoll in the middle of the glen. They kissed ardently, and unconscious of being observed wandered hand in hand to the very spot where Betsy lay concealed, boiling with rage. Unable to control herself for a moment longer she sprang at her husband's lover like a tigress but lo and behold! all she could grasp was the empty green gown. In an instant envy, rage and jealousy fell from Betsy, and love, generosity and tranquillity came upon her. She went to Duncan, clung to him and bestowed upon him lavish affection, and he in turn was overwhelmed with gratitude and love for her. Arms entwined, they made their way homewards, Betsy carefully nursing the green gown. But as they entered the house a nail caught the gown and tore a fragment from it. Betsy's cry of dismay brought one of the ungainly daughters to see what was amiss, and she, on picking up the torn fragment was transformed into a most beautiful woman.

The virtue of the green gown was recognised at once. Betsy always carried a piece over her heart, and she retained her graciousness. Each of the daughters also became charming girls in Strathspey, and never failed to wear a piece of the gown next to their hearts. All were ardently wooed, and all married well and happily, each passing her piece of the precious gown to her daughters, and made their charms as irresistible as her own.

The Raven's Stone

A SHORT distance south west of Loch Insh in Badenoch there used to be a scattering of houses called Balnacraig. The numerous remains of old buildings indicate that in olden days it was a populous township. Its name was derived from the rocky hill lying to the south of the present highway. At the time of the following tale it was densely wooded to the summit, and much favoured by the eagle, raven and wild cat.

In the 14th century Donald Macpherson, the Standard-Bearer to the laird of Invereshie, lived at the foot of Balnacraig in a well-built fortified house, but when the incidents which follow occurred he was an old man and his duties had devolved on *Iain Ban* (fair-haired John), his 19-year-old son who was not only tall, muscular, active and good-looking, but as famous a bowman as he was a swordsman. His handsome figure and countenance, and crop of fair, curly hair were much admired by all the young ladies in the district.

One day when Iain was hunting in Tor Wood, near the head of Loch Insh, he saw a falcon pursuing a heron and striking it to the ground a short distance ahead of him. He walked quickly forward, and as he approached the spot he heard angry voices close at hand. In another moment he came upon a lady on horseback attended by a ghillie, and two of the Laird's foresters. They were disputing the ownership of a falcon which one of the foresters held captive. Seeing Iain the lady cried, "Come, good Sir, and make these men deliver up my falcon." Saluting the lady Iain demanded the reason for the foresters' ungracious behaviour.

"The falcon killed a heron on our chief's land and by law it is his property," replied Murdoch, the senior forester.

"Believe me, Sir," cried the lady, "the heron was sprung in Dunachton Burn which is on my Aunt's land, and my falcon pursued it across the Spey. We were in hot chase and crossed the river at the shallows. Not once did we lose sight of the birds, and therefore both are by right mine."

"Deliver the bird to the lady," commanded Iain. "Judging from what she says, and according to forest law the birds, by right belong to her."

"You know nothing of forest law Mr Standard-Bearer," replied Murdoch. "I will not deliver up the birds, and mind your own business."

In a moment Murdoch and his companion lay flat on their backs from well-aimed blows, and in the melee the falcon escaped and flew to its mistress' wrist.

Meanwhile the foresters had enough and sullenly departed follwed by a stern warning from Iain.

"I will report your insolence to this lady."

"Oh thank you for your gallantry, kind Sir," cried the lady, "Please tell me your name."

"I am Iain Ban, Standard-Bearer to Invereshie at your service fair lady," said Iain proudly drawing himself up to his full six feet of Highland manhood.

"And I am Helen MacIntosh, ward of my Aunt, the Dowager Lady MacIntosh of Dunachton."

"Ah," exclaimed Iain, "Sorry I am to hear it. I would you were of lower degree."

"Why so, my gallant Standard-Bearer?" enquired Helen with laughter in her voice.

"Because, fair lady," said Iain in solemn tones, "I would then crave permission to see you again."

"Fie!" rejoined Helen, "my position is no hindrance. I ride out every day in yonder meadow with Roderick my faithful ghillie."

"Alas," mourned Iain, "the Spey is a barrier between us."

"Nonsense," Helen replied encouragingly, "it is easily forded at the shallows."

When they were parting at the ford, she said, "Goodbye. I know that the game in Tor Wood and the salmon in the Spey will entice you back. We shall soon meet again."

Gallantly Iain kissed the hand held out to him saying, "You are taking my heart with you, fair lady."

"I lost mine in Tor Wood," replied Helen coyly. "Seek for it and keep it."

Iain stood gazing after her enraptured as she rode away, but when at last she disappeared in the Dunachton Woods he heaved a melancholy sigh and returned to Balnacraig.

Helen, in her 25th year, was not, it appears, exactly a beauty because she leaned to the masculine in figure and temperament. She was passionately fond of hunting and other outdoor pursuits. She had the eye of an eagle, a tanned skin and a robust body, and elastic step. She rode fearlessly, and could bring down a deer with bow and arrow, or spear a salmon with consummate skill. To all appearances she and Iain were well-matched.

As Helen had predicted they met again in Tor Wood and continued to meet. Roderick remained discreetly out of sight as they wandered through the woods in sweet dalliance. Then winter came with Spey floods and the river became an impossible barrier between them. The floods were followed by severe black frost freezing the Spey solid. The valley was filled with the merry laughter of numerous skaters, and the secret lovers were able to meet again. However, there was now little privacy and their attachment to each other did not go unnoticed. Their secret was now so transparent that the Dowager was informed. Helen was prohibited from skating, and Iain was sore distracted by her absence and silence. His enquiries of the Dowager's servants met with a frigid response, but one man, more tolerant than the others, gave him kindly advice.

"If you are wise, Balnacraig, keep the Spey always between you and Dunachton."

Iain would normally have made a heated retort but in his present mood he held his tongue for Helen's sake. But he was consumed with anxiety for Helen's safety, knowing the Dowager's reputation of being a tigress when enraged. Quietly he went home to Balnacraig and began to devise means of contacting Helen and snatching her from the claws of "that hell cat" as he called the Dowager. He decided to enlist the aid of *Donnachadh leis an da Ordag* (Duncan with the two thumbs), the blacksmith at Craggan near Balnacraig. Being an important and indispensable member of the community Duncan was completely neutral, and he was as often at Dunachton as he was at Balnacraig. That very morning, it transpired, he had been at Dunachton and Iain feverishly questioned him if he had heard aught of Helen.

"Deed yes Balnacraig," replied Duncan, "she is a close prisoner in her room, and no one is allowed near her."

"Oh Duncan, man," groaned Iain, "sorry I am to hear it. Do you think you could get a letter to her?"

"Och Balnacraig, that would be at peril of my life. Poor Roderick! Only yesterday he lost his head for not letting on about your meetings in the Tor Wood."

"*A' chat bhorbh!*" (the wild cat) exploded Iain. "If I had her here at Balnacraig I would tame her."

"Well," replied Duncan, "the castle is strongly guarded. It would be a hard nut for Invereshie and all his clan to crack."

"Be that as it may," said Iain, "but this is not a clan quarrel. It is my concern and mine only. Surely you could contrive for friendship sake to get a letter to Lady Helen."

"Willingly," agreed Duncan, "but be patient, Balnacraig, hurry might spoil all. Give the old lady time to cool, and my errand will be easier done."

"Time," exploded Iain, "in the meantime the old cat may starve, strangle, or poison my beloved Helen."

"Have no fear," replied Duncan calmly, "Lady Helen has a will of iron and would dirk her before she could do it."

"Ay," agreed Iain, "and I would admire her for it."

"Well," resumed Duncan, "I have no reason to call there again meanwhile. To go back at once would be to raise suspicion. But have your letter ready and I will find a way to deliver it."

Reluctantly Iain agreed. He went home and penned a few guarded words to Helen asking her to inform him of her present position and declaring his undying devotion to her, and his intention, if necessary, to die in her defence.

Day after day Iain scanned the meadows from the heights of Balnacraig for the return of Duncan, but never a sign was there of his messenger. The strain and worry began to tell on him and he started to decline in health. His friends worried, and his father upbraided him for his lack of spirit and action.

"What man," he raged, "when I was a young man I would have carried off my lover by the strength of my arms. If such spirit was lacking a man would have been deemed a coward."

"I don't doubt it," moaned Iain, "and you know, father, that I am no coward, but to force the castle would embroil our chief. That would not be just, and to attempt it alone would be tantamount to putting a halter round my neck and jumping from the highest ramparts of the castle."

"Give up your pining," replied his father with some asperity, "and go to work like a man."

"But how?" cried the poor distraught Iain. "Oh! if I could only see her, and know how she fares I would be more content."

"Well," said his father, "your wish would be granted if only you had the Raven's Stone."

"The Raven's Stone," exclaimed Iain. "Please tell me about it, father."

"The story," continued his father, "is as old as the hills. I had it from your grandfather, and I believe in it. You take the eggs from a raven's nest and after boiling them, return them to the nest. The raven will know the eggs have been tampered with, and will desert the nest and disappear. But on the third day they will return and the male will have a small clear pebble in his beak. If you are on watch you will see him rubbing the eggs with the pebble and they will become fertile again. But you must be constantly on the alert from the time they desert the nest until they return and the rubbing ritual is complete. Now if the watcher can get possession of the pebble he will immediately have the power to make himself invisible at will. All he has to do is put the pebble in his mouth to become invisible, and replace it in his pocket to appear in human form again."

"It is wonderful," cried Iain with sparkling eyes, "but how to test the truth of it."

"Easy," said his foster-brother, Calum, who was present, "I know where to find the nest of a *fitheach*, and with the aid of a rope, I can get into it from the top of a high crag."

"Fine I know the place," said Iain excitedly, "but it will be a tricky and dangerous undertaking, yet it is in a worthy cause and we will attempt it tomorrow."

So on the following morning they set out early with all the necessary tackle, a supply of food and a pan in which to boil the eggs. It was a hazardous exercise but the eggs were secured by the lighter and nimbler foster-brother. They were boiled on a fire of heather roots and duly returned to the nest. In due course, as they lay fully alert out of sight, they saw the birds returning. With loud clamour they hovered over the nest for a brief moment and then flew away to the east.

Now the long vigil commenced. They kept close watch in turn, day and night, and on the morning of the third day they saw the birds fly in and watched as the male rubbed the eggs with a white pebble. Once again the hazardous descent was undertaken and the pebble triumphantly retrieved from the nest. Iain had to test its efficacy straight away, and putting the pebble in his mouth he immediately disappeared from his foster-brother's sight. Knowing precisely where Iain stood he seized him by the arm. Iain was clearly sensible of his foster-brother's touch, and he found that he was also capable of talking to him. As soon as he removed the pebble and stowed it away carefully in his pocket he resumed his form.

In high glee they returned to Balnacraig and recounted their experience to the father and Iain's only sister, Mary. They all agreed that the matter must be kept strictly secret.

"This marvellous pebble would be worth a hundred men in battle," said Iain. "You could destroy your enemies without being seen."

"Ay and in pence too," decided Calum. "You could fill your sporran or larder in safety. I must search for another nest."

"Steady, my boys," cautioned the old man, "I have still to tell you the whole story. You must never use the pebble in the way you are suggesting for its virtues lie in doing good and preventing evil. If used in any other way terrible calamities will follow. Beware! If a drop of blood is shed, or unnecessary violence used when under its spell, its possessor will meet with an awful fate."

"But," said Iain in puzzled tones, "If for example I chanced to be trapped in a narrow passage at Dunachton Castle, how then could I protect myself?"

"Fight manfully," said his father, "but without anger in your heart. Love must always prevail. It is a wonderful and mysterious passion; it is as dew falling from Heaven and any unwarranted hindrance to its operation would be a violation of this wonderful gift of Nature. It was natural love that brought the pebble to the raven's nest. It was love that made you risk your life to possess it, and it is to relieve love in distress that you must use it. Now be off, my son, and luck be with you. If the lady is willing bring her here and we'll get the *naomh duine* (holy man) from Tom Eunan to marry you."

On the east side of Dunachton Castle there was a walled orchard which was used by the residents for recreational strolls. It was divided from the quarters of the lower orders by an ornamental wrought-iron palisade. At one end of the orchard a postern gate gave access to the woods, and it was by this gate that Iain entered the orchard.

To his surprise he saw Helen and her Aunt quite near, but he was immediately dismayed to see two savage-looking mastiffs snarling with bared teeth in their efforts to get through the palisade. He felt like retreating, but when he saw that the ladies were alarmed at the unaccountable behaviour of the dogs he decided to hold on. Obviously the Dowager thought that they had gone mad and shouted loudly for the servants to secure them. This done the ladies continued their walk, quite unconscious of the unseen presence beside them.

Presently the Dowager retired leaving Helen to wander on her own towards a secluded arbour. But Iain reached it before her and deposited a letter in a conspicuous position. What occurred in the bower can only be guessed but that night the lovers arrived back at Balnacraig.

Helen was warmly welcomed, and she was given an assurance by the old man that as it was by her own free will she had left Dunachton to marry his son he would give her all the protection and love he gave his own daughter. Then the old man said to Helen, "Please can you tell us what happened to Donnachadh an da Ordag?"

Sadly Helen told of poor Duncan's fate. He had been detected in the act of delivering a letter from Iain to Helen and he had been brutally murdered.

"By the powers!" the old man cried, "I tell you Lady Macintosh will suffer for this day's work."

"Ah but he was killed unknown to her and his body was buried in the black hole of the sallyport," continued Helen. "When Iain's letter was given to my Aunt, and she was told that the messenger had been killed, her wrath was terrible to behold. She threatened to hang the Captain of the guard, and made me a close prisoner in the tower dungeon for a time."

Whether the Dowager shrewdly guessed, or was informed that Helen was at Balnacraig we do not know, but the very next day she arrived there with a force of fifty well-armed men and demanded that Helen should be immediately restored to her. This, old Balnacraig stoutly refused to do, and the Dowager immediately signalled her men to attack the house. A bloody battle ensued.

Iain gave the magic stone to Helen to use, and keep out of danger while he and the small number of men he had available rushed to the ramparts and with bow and arrow created such death and disarray among the Macintoshes that, few as they were, they were able to sally forth and engage the enemy. Sadly Iain was mortally wounded in the affray, but his assailant was shot through the brain. At the same time a heart-rending cry of anguish was heard above the din of battle, "Dear Iain! I have swallowed the stone."

"*O Dhia gleidh sinn*" (Oh God preserve us) whispered Iain breathing his last. "You will be seen no more Helen, but perhaps it is for the best, because no one can feast his eyes on the treasure I am leaving behind. I am dying, dear Helen, and my last wish is to be buried secretly where we first met in Tor

Wood." Whereupon Iain gave up the ghost.

Meanwhile the Dowager and her remaining followers had retreated in defeat to a distant knoll. Then from Balnacraig came the call of "Revenge! revenge!" It could be heard pursuing the fleeing Macintoshes. The call came from the anguished Helen who was in the vanguard of the pursuit. It was she who killed with every arrow from her bow until only the Dowager and two of her men escaped to Dunachton to tell the tale of being pursued by an invisible fiend.

That night Iain's remains were secretly conveyed to Tor Wood by old Balnacraig and Calum, and reverently laid to rest in a prepared grave. Helen, still invisible, kept watch.

Removing his bonnet the old man said, "Bless thee my only son. Rest from thy wordly toil."

Then Helen was heard to cry, "Wait dear Iain, I am coming to be with you for ever." There was a dull thud at Calum's feet and the sound of a body falling into the grave. Looking down Calum saw a bloody dirk still warm lying at his feet.

Horror-stricken the two men remained speechless for a few moments, then in a voice shaken with grief the old man said, "As I said, I knew that misfortune would follow the misuse of the Raven's Stone. That devoted girl killed her kindred while under its spell, and poor Iain received his fatal wound at the very moment she swallowed it."

Mourning, they filled in the grave, and left no mark by which anyone could tell where Iain and Helen lay.

They say that occasionally on a summer's evening you may hear the plaintive song of an anguished woman on the shore of Loch Insh near Tor Wood.

Insh Church

THE ancient Church of Insh stands on the site of the Chapel of the Swans and dates back to the Celtic Age. The old, battered, early Celtic bronze bell of Insh Church is its greatest treasure. There is a legend attached to it which claims that if it is ever removed from the Church it will always return. It was reputed to have healing properties, and in this connection it was once taken to Perth with the intention of holding it there for all time. The bell, however, kept up the mournful dirge of "*Tom an Eoin, Tom an Eoin*" (the Knoll of the Birds, the knoll on which the Church stands) for so long that it became unbearable, and the bell was restored to its rightful place.

The Church standing on the top of the wooded Tom an Eoin is one of the most interesting in the district. It was dedicated to St. Adamnan, the biographer of St. Columba. The knoll is said to have been sacred to the Druids until the Christian Church ousted the older cult in the Seventh Century. Undoubtedly the knoll was at one time an island. The building itself is reputed to date from the age of the Culdees, and it is quite likely that it did actually have some connection with St. Adamnan himself. It is perhaps the only Scotish church in which divine worship had been held continuously without interruption since the Seventh Century.

In 1960 the Church was completely renovated. The old coloured glass in the windows was replaced with clear glass and the main window had the striking engraving of the St. John's Cross of Iona placed in it. This was the work of the late Helen Turner who was a Lecturer at the College of Art, Edinburgh. At the same time there was also a new pulpit and baptismal front added.

Standing there one can almost sense the rustle of the white robes of Druid priests and priestesses. The Druids included women in their religious orgies, and it is said that the last representative of the Druidic priestesses' died in the district about fifty years ago.

Loch Alvie Church

THE Loch is reputed to have taken its name from St. Ailbhe, whose origins and deeds appear to be more mythical than historic. He first appears as the son of Olchu by his maid servant who ran away before the child was born. She was traced by her lover's master Cronan who, like God Cronus, seemed to have a dislike for children and ordered the infant to be left on the hillside. The mother placed the infant in the shelter of a rock from which he took his name, Ailbhinn, which means a projecting rock. Here tradition says Lochlan, son of Laidir (the strong one) found him being suckled by a wolf. He was then adopted by Lochlan who took him to Ireland and then gave him to a British tribe who baptised him into the Christian faith. Later he is said to have journeyed to Rome, and on returning founded a monastery at Loch Alvie, but this is apochryphal. The cell later bore the name of St. Columba. There is, however, no trace of such a building in or around the loch. His name appears to have been linked with the Irish Bride or St. Briget.

The church and manse stand on a promontory jutting into the loch at the south end. The Church was dedicated to St. Drostan. It is of very early origin, and may have been one of the very early Celtic foundations. Like so many more in the Highlands the Church has suffered great changes. It once had a gallery and a box pew where the Duke and Duchess of Gordon sat, on a higher level than their tenants.

In 1880, through the liberality of the heritors, the Church of Alvie, which is nearly surrounded by Loch Alvie, was largely renewed, and so much improved that it became one of the most attractive little churches in the Highlands.

In the course of excavation work one hundred and fifty skeletons were found beneath the floor lying head to head. There was no evidence of coffins having been used. Speculation has been rife over the years about the identity of these skeletons, but in all probability the bones were those of Highlanders killed in a foray many years before and all laid to rest uncoffined, unshrouded, and unsung within the sacred precincts where possibly they would want to worship. The minister at the time of restoration, the Rev. Mr. Anderson, arranged for their reinternment in the Churchyard and for the granite stone standing over the common grave bearing the inscription:

BURIED HERE
ARE
REMAINS OF 150 HUMAN BODIES
FOUND OCTOBER 1880
BENEATH THE FLOOR OF THIS CHURCH.
WHEN THEY DIED
HOW THEY DIED
TRADITION NOTES NOT
THEIR BONES ARE DUST
THEIR GOOD SWORDS RUST
THEIR SOULS ARE
WITH THE SAINTS WE TRUST

The red granite stone, measuring approximately 3′6″ high by 2′6″ broad, stands about fifty feet from the east gable of the church. Above the inscription a cross has been inscribed.

The recorded list of Ministers dates from 1567. The church was restored several times but notably in 1880 under the Rev. James Anderson (1880–1913).

Was it plague? Were they cut down in battle? The latter may well be the explanation because the Loch is reputed to be haunted by a *Bean Nigheadaireachd* (a phantom washer woman who is seen only by those about to die). Oddly enough no examination of the skeletons seems to have been made, and although the mention of swords in the inscription seems to stregthen the theory that they were cut down in battle there is neither mention of weapons having been found in the mass grave, nor any record of a battle or skirmish in the vicinity.

The Pedlar or Packman's Grave

IN A hollow, a short distance east of the road leading to the farm of Dalnavert at Inshriach, lies the grave of a packman well known in Strathspey, who disappeared suddenly a year or two after the '45 Rebellion. It was known that he left Dalnavert late one evening, but he never arrived at his lodgings at the hamlet of Cock Street which used to exist by the present road east of Tombain. (The foundations of these houses can still be traced.) It was known that he had plenty of money and foul play was suspected. A search party was quickly organised, and the countryside thoroughly searched, but not a trace of him was to be found. Almost twenty years later a shepherd, a complete stranger to the district, was driving sheep across Feshiebridge. Encountering a local well-to-do farmer he asked to be directed to the old drove road which passed through the Forest of Rothiemurchus. The farmer accompanied him some distance to ensure that he was on the right track, and when they reached the edge of the forest the stranger said "I want to go into the woods for a few minutes. If you will be good enough to keep the sheep moving I will soon overtake you".

A short time later the farmer looked back to see if the drover was in sight. There was no sign of him but he did see two men quickly overtaking him. Immediately they seized him, and tied his hands behind his back.

"We have you at last", they said, "Your sins are now known. Will you confess your crimes".

"My God, after all these years," the farmer thought. "Yes", he said, "I killed and robbed the packman. I buried his body and his pack in a hollow in the birch wood at Cock Street".

Astonished, the two men stood looking at him in confusion. Then they were joined by another local farmer who happened to be nearby.

"What's the matter here?" he enquired.

Bewildered, the strangers replied, "This man stole our sheep, but he now confesses to murdering a packman".

"No", said the newcomer, "he is not guilty of stealing your sheep, but I well remember the murder at Cock Street and he may possibly be the culprit".

"It is a judgement come upon me", moaned the accused, "I will make full confession, and suffer for a terrible crime from which all I got was £20. As far as the sheep are concerned the thief escaped into the wood when he became aware that you were at his heels. I was only directing him on the right track through Rothiemurchus."

The sheep had been stolen from Killiehuntly near Kingussie, but the thief was never discovered. The murderer was taken to the Inn at Feshiebridge to await instructions from Inverness, but he cheated the gallows by dying that night.

The Crafty Alvie Tailor

THERE is a small, nameless burn flowing into Loch Alvie near the north end, and thereby hangs a tale. The burn is the boundary between the Alvie and Seafield Estates. Beside it are the ruins of a cottage. On the west side of the burn there lived a tailor, well known for his craftmanship and wit. He was something of a poet and bard, and as he travelled round the district plying his needle he delighted his audience with impromptu ballads, which were couched in language uncomplimentary to his landlord. The laird was not amused, and after a particularly scurrilous effusion he was evicted from his cottage.

Not to be outdone the wily tailor approached the neighbouring laird, a man of some humour, and asked for permission to occupy an empty cottage on the east side of the burn, exactly opposite the one from which he was being evicted. With some guile he added that rhymes in praise of a kind laird were as easy to compose as quatrains couched in derogatory terms. Much amused the new laird immediately agreed and the wily stitch and ballad-monger flitted the few hundred yards from the one cottage to the other.

Rising above the loch was the conical hill called The Tor, on top of which is a ninety-foot high pillar dedicated to the memory of the Fifth Duke of Gordon. It was erected in 1840 and bears the inscription in Gaelic, Latin and English. There is another smaller monument on The Tor, erected by the Marquis of Huntly in 1815 to perpetuate the memory of the Highland soldiers who fell at the Battle of Waterloo.

The Stewarts of Kincardine

ON the hill above Loch Pityoulish there is an outstanding rocky height called *Creag Chaisteal* (Castle Rock). On it are the remains of a huge fort, now just a heap of stones. The diameter is about twenty-seven feet, and the walls about eleven feet thick. They were built dry: there is no evidence of vitrification. It was probably a watch tower in its day. On the moor below the remains of cairns and hut circles are to be found. On one massive, flat stone there are four cup marks.

On the face of Pityoulish Hill a projecting crag is called the Baron's Chair. Here the Stewart Barons of Kincardine were wont to sit and view their fair lands below with pride. Well might the Barons have echoed the sentiments of Ulysses who loved Ithaca so dearly, not because it was broad and large, not because it was small, but "because it was his own".

At the east end of Loch Pityoulish, near the march between Kincardine and Rothiemurchus lies the hollow where Shaw Mór of Rothiemurchus waylaid a party of Comyns and slew them to a man. The mounds of their graves may still be seen.

At low water the remains of an island appear. It may well have been a *crannog*, an artificial island where, when danger threatened, the people could take refuge.

It was believed that the loch harboured an *each uisge* (a water horse) which in defiance of tradition was black in colour and lived in a sunken crannog. One day the black horse appeared to the young heir to the Barony of Kincardine as he played with other children by the side of the loch. The horse was decked out with silver saddle, silver bridle and silver reins. The boys grasped the reins and mounted, and the horse galloped off with them and plunged into the loch. Only the young heir who had the presence of mind to cut his fingers free of the ensnaring reins with his *sgian dubh* lived to tell the tale.

The first Baron of Kincardine was Walter, the third natural son of Alexander Stewart, Earl of Buchan, the *Ridire Ruadh* (Red Knight), but better known as the infamous Wolf of Badenoch. Walter was granted a Charter of the Lands of Kincardine from King Robert III at Perth in 1400.

After quite a long succession of Stewart Barons, many of them notable men, the last Baron was Donald who had a son by his second wife Barbara, a daughter of John Stuart of Giuslich. He was the only son of the marriage, and this was the celebrated John Roy Stewart. His mother was fifty-five when he was born in the year 1700 at the Knock of Kincardine. He was a fine, healthy youngster with a shock of red hair by which he became affectionately known as *Iain Ruadh* (Red John). He grew in stature and strength of character with the years, and when he came of age he joined the army. He served for several years as Lieutenant and Quarter Master in the Scots Greys until 1740. He had hopes, along with his close friend, Nigel Grant of Dalrachney, of obtaining a Commission in the Black Watch which had been raised in 1730. His application for a Commission was surprisingly refused and, irritated by the rebuff, he retired from the King's service and, casting in his lot with the Jacobites, moved to France and served in Flanders. The night before the Battle of Fontenoy he visited Lewis Grant of Auchterblair in the opposing English camp, and spent a happy evening with him and other friends. The next day they were in bloody conflict.

On 19th August 1745 the *Bratach Ban*, the White Banner of the Jacobites, was unfurled at Glenfinnan. Immediately the news reached him John Roy returned to Scotland and joined Prince Charles Edward at Blair Castle. He had admirable qualities of devotion and trustworthiness, and the culture and military skills which he had acquired from service at home and abroad endeared him to all who knew him, but in particular to Prince Charles Edward. He referred to him whimsically as "The Body", and frequently consulted him.

In Edinburgh he raised what became known as the Edinburgh Castle Regiment, and put it to good service in the Jacobite cause. In the north his skill and resource, and his intimate knowledge of the country were of inestimable value to the Prince, and it is observed that in almost every order the Edinburgh Regiment was singled out for patrol and scouting duties. At Culloden it formed part of the front line commanded by John Roy himself, and suffered dire losses. One of Cumberland's officers remarking on John Roy's valour said, "If all the Highlanders had fought as well as the officer with the red hair and the little hand the issue might have been different." He emerged from the '45 Rebellion in the words of Chambers in his *History of the Rebellion* as "the beau-ideal of a clever Highland Officer". The colours of his Regiment, known as the Green Flag of Kincardine, were saved from falling into the hands of Government troops and brought back by the Standard Bearer to the family home at Pityoulish. Every year during his lifetime the Standard Bearer took the battle-scarred banner to the summit of Cairngorm and there unfurled it in the breeze as a tribute to his gallant Colonel and a gesture of defiance to Butcher Cumberland, and all that he stood for. It is believed by some that the banner may still be in existence somewhere.

During the rout which followed he made his way to Ruthven where remnants of the broken clans had gathered round the Prince. When they dispersed he disconsolately sought refuge at Kincardine, outlawed with a price on his head; but his whereabouts were never betrayed. One of his refuges was a cave on Craigowrie above Tulloch, and from the loophole in this retreat he had a wide view of all movements in the valley below. It is still called John Roy's cave, but is extremely difficult to find. In one of his songs he speaks of bathing a badly sprained ankle sitting under the waterfall called *Slugan an Eas*, weary and sad but still hopeful of better days. When Kincardine became too hot he crossed into Glenmore where he had good friends, but on the advice of an Irish informer the Redcoats followed. They were resting at a certain spot when a young fair-haired boy, carrying a silver-rimmed cog of milk came along the path the soldiers were following. "What is your name and where are you going?" their officer enquired. "Peter Bell", replied the boy, "and I am going to my father who is working in the wood." Feigning curiosity, as if he had never seen such a thing before, he kept on handling their drum which lay on the path. Noticing his apparent interest one of the soldiers said, "That is a pretty cog, what will you take for it?" "This bonny thing", said the boy and, picking it up, beat out a loud tatoo, and followed it with a well-known tune:

> *Bi falbh 's na fuirich*
> *Bi falbh, bi falbh,*
> *Na tig a nochd tuillidh*
> *Tha'n toir a tighinn thugad*
> *Na tig a nochd tuillidh*
> *Bi falbh, bi falbh.*

> Be off and stay not
> Away, away,
> Return not tonight
> The pursuers are near
> Return not tonight
> Away, away.

The sound of the drum came clearly to the ears of John Roy. He recognised the message, for he had taught the boy himself, and he was instantly alert. "Whatever that drum is, the beat is Peter Bell's", he said, and instantly sped eastwards through the Pass of Revoan to the Braes of Abernethy and Balnagown, and from there to Badaneden where he rested for a few days. One day when he was singing and telling stories to a little child, Mary Grant of Auchernack came rushing in to warn him of the approach of Redcoats. With great presence of mind the good wife threw an old ragged plaid over him and handed him a staff. In the guise of a poor beggar John Roy hirpled his way along the hillside until he came to the forest, and then with all speed made for a known shelter near Connage on the other side of the hill. In a gorge there, at the foot of a cliff shaded by scrubby trees, there may still be seen the long smooth slab under which he lay wrapped in his plaid on a bracken bed. A little girl cautiously brought him food, and when the coast was clear he would climb the hill to Cannage to talk with his good friend John Stewart. News of what was happening was regularly brought to him, and when a command was received from the Prince to join him he took leave of his good friends at Badaneden, and gave John Stewart his sporran as a keepsake. He then set out westwards to meet Prince Charles at Cluny's Cage on Ben Alder. As he passed through the homeland he loved so much he must have felt in his inner heart that he was seeing it for the last time. On the 14th September 1746 the Prince's party stealthily made their way westwards to Borrowdale, and on 20th September boarded the frigate that awaited them and sailed for France.

John Roy Stewart never saw Kincardine again. He died at St. Omer in France in 1752.

Besides being a valiant soldier and a man of high principles John Roy Stewart was a poet of no mean standard and composed a number of hymns and songs in Gaelic. His *Lament for Lady MacIntosh*, the predecessor of the courageous Lady MacIntosh of the '45, was remarked upon as having an "intenseness of feeling which seems to resolve itself into the element which it contemplates". His two poems on Culloden, *Catha Chullodair*, glow with feeling for Prince Charles, and indignation and passionate grief for the wrongs and savagery inflicted upon his followers. Some of his songs are light and humorous and broadly sympathetic like Burns'.

Kincardine Church

THE ancient Church situated at the west end of Tulloch, not far from the east bank of the Spey, and between Boat of Garten and Coylumbridge, is still used regularly for worship. It is pre-Reformation, and although it was rebuilt in fairly recent times part of the foundations date from the 12th Century.

On the east wall there is a leper's "peep", or narrow window now glassed because of draughts, for lepers and others who were not allowed to enter the Church to look in, and hear the minister's discourse. There is a tradition that when the lairds of Tulloch and Kincardine decided to build the Church a dispute arose about the exact site. Each wanted the Church on his land. Eventually tiring of the dispute the Laird of Tulloch set about gathering suitable stones, and had his men dump them on a site which he had selected on Tulloch land. But each time a heap was gathered the stones mysteriously transferred themselves to the site of the present Church. At last it was accepted that divine intervention was taking place, and the Church was built on its present site.

It was at one time called *Eaglais Thomhaldidh*. The name is obscure but *Thomhaldidh* might well have been one of St. Columba's messengers. There is a well of the same name nearby, and also a knoll of that name further east of Tulloch.

In the 15th century the Church was the scene of a dreadful tragedy. The Chief of the Grants of Rothiemurchus, along with his son, were waylaid by their hereditary enemies, the Comyns, and murdered not far from the Church. The Grants, accompanied by their allies the Stewarts of Kincardine, pursued the Comyns who, finding themselves outnumbered, took refuge in the Church where they were secure and impossible to dislodge. The difficulty was eventually solved when one of the Grants fired a burning arrow into the thatched roof. Soon the building was a mass of flames and the Comyns all perished, except for one man of huge stature who succeeded in breaking out, but he was instantly cut down.

In 1885, while digging in the churchyard for the foundations of a tombstone, the workmen discovered a grave completely surrounded by a masonry wall. Inside, the skeleton of a woman was revealed along with her rusted spurs. The skeleton was assumed to be that of the Fifth Baron of Kincardine who lived in the 15th Century. He was twice married, his second wife being a daughter of Cameron of Lochiel. When she was about to be married her father asked her what she would like for her tocher, or dowry. She replied that she had little use for silver, but would be glad of a few men of her own clan to take with her into the strange country. So she was provided with twelve strapping young Camerons as her bodyguard. In Kincardine they were known as the bonnetless lads, owing to their habit of going about bare headed, instead of wearing the customary blue bonnet. But she was not happy at Kincardine. She pined for Lochaber, and before many years had passed she died. On her deathbed she was greatly troubled to think of being buried so far from her kinsfolk. Her pride was also hurt at the thought of having to take second place beside her husband. To comfort her the Baron said she would be laid to rest on Lochaber ground. But owing to the troubled times, and the difficulty in transporting her coffin for such a long distance, the Baron kept his promise by building a special tomb, and the body was laid in earth and brought from Lochaber.

The power of the Church over the people in those days is unbelievable to us today and the Session records of the Church are revealing. Much that was good in the people is recorded, but evil predominates. Sunday after Sunday the black calendar runs on, and at almost every Session meeting there are cases to be recorded of evil-doing, and the consequent rebuking of the culprits in front of the congregation.

The last recorded case in the Kincardine Session records reads as follows: "Clach Glass of Kincardine 16th August 1761. The Session having received the following dismal and shocking report, viz:- that a male child lately born was found yesterday by the Fishers drowned anent the house of Kinchirdy in Spey and the pool commonly called Pol Marstack. The Session having taken this affair under consideration have appointed a meeting at the place on Wednesday next the nineteenth current to make the search possible, as far as law will, for the mother of the said child, by calling all young women unmarried, under fifty years and maidens of above fifteen years, that they may be seen and searched, if there by any New milk in their breasts, whereby any of them may be suspected to be the mother of the child, and appoint the minister to intimate this from the pulpit after divine service this day."

In the ancient graveyard lies the dust of an historical character. The tombstone bears the inscription now so weathered that it is barely legible - "Sacred to the memory of Walter Stuart, grandson of Robert II and his family who possessed the Barony of Kincardine 1374 - 1683. Also of H.C. Stuart M.A., Vicar of Wragley, one of their descendants who died 16th September 1884. To fulfil his wish this memorial is erected."

It is to be deplored that no interest has been shown in having the lettering of this interesting and historical inscription rechiselled, but steps are being taken to bring the matter to the attention of the relevant authorities.

This Walter Stuart, First Baron of Kincardine, was the fourth natural son of Alexander Stewart, Earl of Buchan and Lord of Badenoch, better known for his nefarious deeds as the Wolf of Badenoch. He was knighted for valour after the Battle of Harlaw 1411. He was also known as *Ridire Ruadh* (the Red Knight) on account of his red hair.

At the entrance gates to the Churchyard there is an ancient laburnum with a girth of eighty-six inches at three feet from ground level. The main trunk has now been split for many years and leans outwards. Preservative measures might be taken by scraping down the hollow to the bare wood and then coating it with a mastic fungicide and filling the hole with cement. It might well last if treated for another hundred years. Its age might be several hundred years. It is interesting to note that the seeds from this tree are still viable. Also in the Churchyard the dwarf elder grows. It is not found anywhere else in the district. It was known to the folk as the Baron Lady's Flower, because it is believed that the seeds were brought with the soil from Lochaber where it is common.

The Stewarts of Glenmore

IN the early 18th century Glenmore was the home of Robert Stewart of Fincastle who became Keeper of the Forest for the Duke of Gordon. He was a subaltern in Argyll's Regiment when Captain Robert Campbell of Glen Lyon received his instructions on 12th February 1692. "You are hereby ordered to fall upon the rebells, the MacDonalds of Glencoe, and put all to the sword under seventy . . . ."

Robert Stewart, to his infinite credit, was one man who refused to be a party to this blackest of crimes in all the turbulent history of the Highlands. Because of his ability and courage he was chosen as one of the party who was to commit the infamous deed of extirpation of an unsuspecting and hospitable community. He refused to have any hand in it despite dire threats on his life. He threw up his commission and, fleeing northwards, sought the protection of the Duke of Gordon. The Duke readily agreed, but as he could not give him a commission he appointed him Keeper of Glenmore Forest which, in those days, was a position of considerable importance. In a Forest Land Act of James VI it was declared that Keepers of Forests should have power and jurisdiction to convene before them transgressors of the Laws, and try them by inquest.

Robert Stewart was a tried and trusted servant. He married a local lady and had a large family. Five of his daughters married respectable local tacksmen, and Robert himself is said to have lived to be over one hundred years. He was succeeded by his son James who was well-educated and so shrewd and capable that he was able to save quite a bit of money. His contemporaries, jealous of his success and relative

138

wealth, jumped to the conclusion that a local character called the *Claddach* had told James about dreaming of a pot of gold under a certain stone. James had laughed and said with a careless shrug, "Who minds a dream?" But, they decided, James had craftily taken note of the *Claddach*'s dream and had retrieved the *ulaidh* (treasure) from under the stone. The truth was, of course, that James had thrived by his own thrift and industry. He had three sons and one daughter who married Stewart of the Knock, one of the Baron of Kincardine's clan. The sons prospered like their father and were much favoured by the Duke of Gordon. Before the venerable James died on Christmas Day 1795 his sons were in possession of the best farms in the district — John at Pityoulish, Charles at the Knock and Patrick at Achgourish.

In his last years, because of his long, white beard and patriarchal appearance, James was well-known throughout Badenoch and Strathspey as the *Fear Liath* (Grey Man), not to be confused with the *Fear Laith Mor*, the *bochdan* of Ben MacDhui.

John of Pityoulish, a notable hunter and fisher, was reckoned to be one of the finest-looking men in the whole of Strathspey. In 1792 he was appointed a Deputy Lieutenant of Inverness-shire, an honour conferred normally on large estate proprietors. His marriage was a romance gleefully recounted by the people of the district. Mary Grant of Kinchurdy, on the opposite bank of the Spey, was a beautiful girl with a string of wooers to her bow. One ardent swain was the Parish minister who had found much favour with her father. But Mary's heart was with the gallant Pityoulish, and on an occasion when the minister was preaching at Kincardine and staying overnight at Kinchurdy he was awakened in the morning by some stir outside. Looking out of the window he was surprised to see what appeared to be a wedding party on the far bank of the Spey. Little did he guess that Pityoulish, like young Lochinvar, had carried off the not unwilling lady, and along with his brother had made a king's chair for her by locking their hands and carried her safely across the Spey. The Parish Minister of Duthil was in the ploy and married them straightaway.

Pityoulish had one son and two daughters whose sons had a distinguished career in the army. Charles of Knock had two sons who fought with gallantry in the Peninsular War. John, who was a Captain in the 53rd Regiment, was popularly called the *Oithear Mor* (the Big Officer) because of his stature and strength. He apparently had no equal for strength in Strathspey, and this was demonstrated with two boulders which lie near the entrance gates at Achernack. They were called *Clachan Neart* (stones of power or strength). Some strong fellows could lift the smaller of the two and toss it over the dyke but only the *Oithchear Mor* could toss both over the dyke as if they were marbles.

Pityoulish lived to a great age. In the last year of his life he made a pilgrimage to his beloved Glenmore. He came to *Sithean Dubh da Choimhead* (Fairy Knolls of the Double Outlook) above the Green Loch in the Pass of Revoan by sunrise, and like Domhnull Mor, sat for a while gazing about him deep in thought; then he came to Riluig and breakfasted. From thence by the south shore of Loch Morlich: past the *Rabhag*, the Osprey Tree, he slowly made his nostalgic way until he came to the west end of Loch Morlich, and crossing the Luinneag here went home to Pityoulish to die.

An amusing story is told of an Engish guest of the Duke of Gordon at Kinrara who expressed a great ambition to stalk and kill a stag. "You'll have to see Pityoulish about that," the Marquis told him. The Englishman replied that all he required was the Marquis's permission. As far as Stewart was concerned he would handle him all right. To which the Marquis replied, "You may try, but I'm mistaken if you don't repent it."

When the bold gentleman arrived in Glenmore he was immediately challenged by Pityoulish and unwisely adopted a haughty approach to his business. "What is that to you? I come from Kinrara." Couteously Pityoulish asked him if he had a note from the Marquis to that effect, but, of course, he had not bothered about such a precaution. "If you have no letter," said Pityoulish, "you have no right to be here. Hand over your gun." The Englishman had no sooner refused than he found himself on his back in the heather, the gun wrested from him. Fuming with mortification, he returned to Kinrara and complained bitterly about such cavalier treatment at the hands of the Marquis's Forest Keeper. But the Marquis just laughed and said unsympathetically, "Did I not tell you how it would be?"

Rothiemurchus

THE derivation of the name Rothiemurchus is obscure. Professor Blackie claimed that it was derived from the Gaelic *Rath Mhór Ghiuthais* (Plain of the Big Firs). This was apt in early times but it is not acceptable to all contemporary Gaelic scholars.

There is peace and tranquility in the Forest of Rothiemurchus today but before the 12th century it had a turbulent history. Much history has been written about the Overlords of those times who, by their power, held the local clans and their septs in subjugation, and they need only to be mentioned briefly here.

Shaw in his *History of the Province of Moray* which at one time embraced the best part of Inverness-shire, Nairnshire and part of Banffshire referred to the ancient Lordship of Badenoch thus: "I cannot trace the possession of the country higher than the Cummines, Lords of Badenoch, who, I doubt not, were Lords of it in the 12th or beginning of the 13th century."

It appears that agreements were reached between Walter Comyn and the Bishop of Moray in connection with these lands between 1223 and 1224 and again in 1225. According to other records the Comyns, Cumins, Cummines, or in modern times Cummings, came over with William the Conqueror in the 11th century. Other historians claim that they arrived in Scotland in the reign of David I (1124/1153), but there is doubt about the exact time and manner in which they became one of the most wealthy and influential families in Scotland.

The first Comyn to be recognised as Lord of Badenoch was in the reign of Alexander III (1249-86). They were a turbulent and haughty race, and ruled their territory with a rod of iron until Robert the Bruce came to the throne in 1306. He reduced them to such an extent that they were no longer a power in the land, although nests of the vipers did remain as a thorn in the flesh of some of the lesser clans in the district, in particular the Shaws of Rothiemurchus.

Bruce bestowed the title Earl of Moray on his nephew Thomas Randolph, and at the same time created him Overlord of all the lands in Badenoch and Rothiemurchus previously held by the Comyns. Randolph and his successors appear to have held all these lands until around 1370 when they were bestowed on the Stewarts who were closely allied to Bruce. Bruce's grandson became Robert II, the first Stewart to ascend the Scottish throne. In 1379 he appointed Alexander, his fourth natural son, as his lieutenant from the southern extremities of Badenoch to the Pentland Firth. Alexander was variously known as Alasdair Mór Mac an Righ (Big Alexander, Son of the King), sometimes the *Ridire Ruadh* (Red Knight) on account of his red hair, but more commonly because of his wolfish nature, buck-teeth and profiligacy as the notorious and evil Wolf of Badenoch.

He had a residence in the Castle of Loch an Eilean which had been built by the Comyns, but his main residence was at Ruthven Castle which had also been built by the Comyns on a green mound opposite Kingussie. Here in security, and presuming on his connection with the Crown, his tyrannical rule spread terror and devastation in all the surrounding countryside.

In a dispute with the Bishop of Moray in 1380 over his annexation of the lands of Rothiemurchus and other nefarious deeds, he was forced to acknowledge the Overlordship of the Bishop in Badenoch and Rothiemurchus. The exactions of the Church irked him to such a degree that he sacked and burned Forres and Elgin and desecrated Elgin Cathedral so severely that it too was demolished. He was excommunicated, but later sought absolution by doing penance and making reparations. He died in 1394 and was buried in Dunkeld Cathedral. His weathered tombstone carries the barely decipherable inscription "Hic jacet Alexander Senescallus Filius Roberti regisScotorum et Elizabethae more dominus de Buchan et Badenoch qui obiit A.D. 1394."

Alexander was succeeded by his eldest natural son, Duncan who, it appears, had inherited his father's vices and profligacy. He was the last Stewart Overlord in Badenoch and Rothiemurchus of whom there is any written or traditional account.

The lands which had once more reverted to the Crown were bestowed upon the first Earl of Huntly in 1452 as feudal superior in recognition of his services to King James II, and continued in the hands of the Gordons for the next four hundred years. They were the last of the all-powerful Overlords in Badenoch and Rothiemurchus. Compared to their predecessors their rule in the district was benign.

But what of the less powerful Chiefs and Lairds in the district who had been under the tyranny of the wealthy Norman Barons for so long? The Macintoshes of Moy, Rothiemurchus and other lands derived, it is said, from Feradach Fada, a son of Feradach, King of Dalriada who died in 697. It was all very obscure, however, and it was not until the 12th Century that the question of lineage became clearer, and not definite until charters to land were granted in the 15th Century. The earliest known ancestry was traced to Shaw MacDuff, third son of the Earl of Fife who was of Royal descent.

The derivation of the name Shaw, or Seath in Gaelic, is likewise obscure but Shaw MacDuff was the progenitor of the Macintoshes by taking the name *Mac an tòisich*, meaning son of the Chief or Thane. Shaw Macintosh died in 1179. The Macintoshes of Rothiemurchus took the name of Shaw, but it was not until the 17th Century that the name came into common use as a surname.

Ferquhand the Third Macintosh Chief had an agreement with the Bishop of Moray in 1215 whereby he was quoted as Seneschal of Badenoch and thus began the Macintoshes' long connection with Badenoch and Rothiemurchus. He was succeeded by his nephew Shaw in 1240. Shaw had obtained a lease of Rothiemurchus in 1236. The feu right was not, however, obtained until 1464. Ferquhand the Fifth Chief succeeded in 1265 and lived at Rothiemurchus. His only son, Angus, was a minor when his father was killed in a fierce encounter with the Comyns and as a result of this action the Comyns seized all the Macintosh lands and started a feud that was to last for two centuries.

In the meantime young Angus and his devoted nurse, Janet Shaw, escaped the holocaust to the hills and eventually reached Strathardle in Perthshire where she sought asylum for the boy with the Baron of Strathardle, a close friend of his father. He assured her that Angus would be reared with as much care as one of his own. The devoted nurse returned to Rothiemurchus only to find her family and friends in servitude to the hated Cuimeaneach.

The years rolled on drearily, but unknown to the usurpers the child, now grown to young manhood, and tutored by Strathardle in the cruel fate of his lands and people, and the steps he must take to redeem them, secretly visited Rothiemurchus in the dead of night with a strong bodyguard to see for himself the real state of affairs. He lost no time in contacting his old nurse at her cottage. Her door was heavily bolted. When he announced himself his voice was unrecognisable after so many years and despite all protestations she remained suspicious, though hopeful that it really was her former charge. Still unconvinced she announced that she would put him to the test.

"Breathe through the keyhole", she commanded, "I shall know your breath."

Astonished at such an extraordinary means of identification young Shaw decided to try a hoax. Beckoning to one of his followers he indicated to him in sign language to breathe through the keyhole. Rejection was instant — *"Bi falbh, bi falbh a chealgare, cha'n eil gaoth t-ainealach ach fuaraidh an aite anail mhilis bhlasda leanaban mo ghaoil"* (Be off, be off, deceitful wretch, the odour of your breath is but cold in comparison with the sweet breath of my own beloved child).

Angus was immediately repentant, and could no longer endure trifling with one who remembered him so vividly. He explained the deception and when he breathed through the keyhole he was immediately recognised and greeted with open arms.

That night the old lady insisted that they kill her only cow and feast themselves. They learned from Janet that the Cummings were away on a foray but were expected back the following day. Shaw at once decided to intercept them, and if possible extinguish them root and branch, and regain for himself the heritage which they had for so long and so unjustly possessed. Their plans were made and by daylight they had, on Janet's advice, taken up a strategic position on the Calart Hill at the eastern extremity of Rothiemurchus. Janet herself insisted on being a party to the ambush because, as she pointed out, if the day went against them she would surely be killed by the Comyns.

She then made her way to a neighbouring hill which had a commanding view of the valley and the road by which the Comyns must come. Soon she saw the first party of Comyns approaching with a *creach* of cattle, and when they reached the spot where Angus and his men lay in hiding she called out the watchword: "Tha nan gobhair air a' Chalart" (The goats are on the Calart).

In a moment the ambushers swept down the hill and slaughtered the first group of unsuspecting Comyns to a man. As each company of Comyns arrived driving separate lots of cattle they also were ruthlessly exterminated until not a single enemy remained alive. All were buried at the same spot at the east end of Loch Pityoulish which to this day is called *Lag nan Chuimeaneach* (The Hollow of Comyns or Cummings). The green grassy mounds remain as evidence of the slaughter.

The power of the Comyns had been broken earlier but enough enclaves remained to create occasional conflicts. But for the moment their strength was broken and Angus regained his birthright. His widowed mother had survived the brutalities of the Comyns and had now remarried.

Her husband was a Southron called Dallas with whom Angus had a relationship which, if not warm, was at least tolerant. This continued for some time but the relationship

146

cooled. At a gathering of friends Dallas unwisely made a disparaging remark to Angus whose pride was instantly wounded. He boiled with fury but held his hand until later, at a quiet spot on their way home, he drew his dagger and stabbed Dallas in the heart. That spot is still called *Lag an Dalasaich* (The Hollow of The Ferry). Not content with that he severed Dallas' head and when he arrived home presented it to his mother exclaiming:

"There it is for you, take it, the head of your blackguardly husband."

The poor woman was distraught at the ghastly sight, and shocked that her own son could have been guilty of such a crime and injustice to herself. She cursed him and warned that she would leave no stone unturned to bring him to justice. She succeeded in rousing the anger of the people to such an extent that Shaw was outlawed and forced to go into hiding. Soon after this he died and once more Rothiemurchus reverted to the Crown.

In the late 16th Century Sir John Grant of Freuchie (later Castle Grant) granted to Patrick, his second son, a feu charter of the lands of Muckerach, Dulnan Bridge, where, in 1598, Patrick built a castle which was never a castle in the true sense of the word but merely a castellated mansion with a tower. Shortly afterwards Sir John acquired the lands of Rothiemurchus and, redeeming Muckerach, settled Patrick at Rothiemurchus as the First Chief of Grant to rule those lands. The present Grants of Rothiemurchus are directly descended from him.

For a long time Muckerach was a picturesque ruin. The door lintel inscribed with the date 1598, three antique crowns and three wolf heads (the family arms) and the words "IN GOD IS ALL MY TREST" was taken to Rothiemurchus and built into the farmhouse of The Dell where it remains to this day. In recent years Muckerach was rebuilt and is once again a fine mansion.

Patrick's hold on Rothiemurchus was tenuous in the early stages on account of the claim by the Chief of Macintosh that he held the hereditary title to it. The Shaws who derived from the Macintoshes had been in occupation, of course, but under the patronage of The Macintosh. Acrimony and numerous skirmishes occurred and continued, but Patrick grimly held on to his property, and his descendants have retained the lands of Rothiemurchus to this day without the loss of one square yard except for what they themselves may have disposed of in recent years.

The Doune of Rothiemurchus was the family seat but Loch an Eilean Castle was restored by Patrick as a safe retreat in the event of continuing serious troubles with the Macintoshes and Shaws. It was uncomfortable for him that the Chief of the ousted Shaws continued to live at the Dell of Rothiemurchus.

The little island which gave the Loch its name was originally a *crannog*. It was a secure retreat for generations of primitive inhabitants who lived in wicker huts on crude platforms. Finally it formed a foundation for a feudal stronghold of considerable dimensions. Tradition asserts that it was originally built by the Red Comyn.

Patrick also destroyed the Shaws' ancient fortress on the Doune Hill. Sometime between 1520 and 1525 Loch an Eilean Castle was the scene of a grim revenge after Lachlan Macintosh of Dunachton had been murdered by a near kinsman. Lachlan's clansmen pursued the murderer and his band to the castle and put every man to the sword. Another account claims that the culprits were chained in the castle until 1531 when, after trial before the Earl of Moray, they were found guilty. Malcolm Macintosh the ringleader was summarily beheaded and quartered. His two companions, both Davidsons, were first tortured then hanged and quartered, and their heads set on poles at the scene of the crime.

A notable event took place at Loch an Eilean after the Grants took possession. In 1651 James Grant of Rothiemurchus married Grace Macintosh of Killachy. She was a big woman and on this account she was called Griseil or Giorsal Mhór (Big Grace). In 1690 after the disastrous Battle of Cromdale the remnants of the defeated adherents of James II under General Buchan fled westwards to Loch an Eilean for refuge and laid seige to the castle. They were successfully repulsed by the Rothiemurchus men. The bullets for the volley of musketry which greeted the invaders were cast by Griseil Mhór. The castle was later vacated and fell into a state of decay. Since those far-off days the castle has stood a picturesque ruin. The stumps of the fir trees from which the timbers of the castle were cut may still be found.

An old tradition persists that a zig-zag path leads from the door of the castle to the shore but even at the lowest water no indication of a causeway has ever been found. Here the osprey regularly nested but as a result of constant harassment they ceased to visit their old home and have not yet returned.

When the Shaws reigned at the Doune of Rothiemurchus they were waited upon by an elf called the *Bodach an Duin* (Goblin of the Doune). When the Grants displaced the Shaws the *bodach* also departed chanting a Gaelic valedictory rhyme, and took upon himself to guard the grave of the last Shaw Chief of Rothiemurchus, Seath Mór Sgor Fhiaclach.

He must, however, have been taken off guard on at least two occasions. On the flat stone commemorating the death of Seath Mór Sgor Fhiaclach in 1405 there are five round stones shaped like cheeses which are said to have come from the large prehistoric mound behind The Doune. Attached to them is a prophecy that anyone who moved a single stone would die. It was believed locally that the prophecy was fulfilled when a young footman in the service of the Duke of Bedford, who had a lease of The Doune for a period, scoffed at such superstition and removed one of the stones. A few days later when attempting to ford the Spey a sudden spate swept him off his feet and he was drowned. In 1982 there was much local concern when on two occasions the stones were again removed.

Not to be outshone by any Shaw goblin the Grants had two faithful retainers in the shape of brownies. They reaped and threshed and performed Herculean tasks for the family, and all they demanded in payment was a jug of milk and some bannocks left for them in the kitchen every night. They were, in fact, so indispensable that they took it in turn to lean over the Laird's shoulder as he played at the dambrod and advise his next move.

In time, however, only one remained and he also disappeared because of the Laird's thoughtlessness. One night when he started to clean the pots and pans he was making such a clamour that the normally placid Laird found the noise unbearable. Groaning with annoyance and muttering to himself, "That Brownie!" he got up and went downstairs. "Stop that awful noise" he roared, whereupon the Brownie in high dudgeon disappeared and was never seen again. Next morning the household rose to a scene of disarray in the kitchen: dirty pots and pans strewn all over the place, chimneys sooty and hearths unswept. After that, cream would disappear from the dairy under mysterious circumstances. A watch was kept, but the culprit was never discovered. Naturally, the Brownie was blamed.

The Shaws insisted on burying their Chief beside his forebears in Rothiemurchus Churchyard. The Grants objected but the Shaws and their Macintosh allies mustered a strong force and laid the Chief in the family burial ground. At night the Grants lifted the remains and took them to Dalnavert at Inshriach where the Chief's widow lived. They propped the body against the door but the following day the Shaws reinterred it at Rothiemurchus. It was again lifted and taken to Dalnavert but this time the Shaws reinterred it deep under the Laird's seat in the church where it was allowed to lie unmolested. But it was some satisfaction to the Laird of Grant that he could sit and stamp his feet on his old enemy!

John and Giorsal were succeeded by their son Patrick who was popularly known as MacAlpine. He was a notable Laird and a striking figure; tall, handsome, prodigiously strong and proud to be named in honour of Rob Roy, the famous freebooter and Chief of the MacGregors of Balquhidder who was a firm friend of the Grants, and a frequent visitor at Rothiemurchus. MacAlpine, who usually travelled with a bodyguard, was known far beyond the bounds of Rothiemurchus and Strathspey. His bodyguard consisted of twenty-four gaily dressed young clansmen who accompanied him round the country dispensing justice and administering punishment, not only in Rothiemurchus but further afield. MacAlpine himself was both judge and jury, and his men saw to it that his verdicts were summarily executed. Even when the verdict was death the justice of the sentence was never questioned.

The Macintoshes and Shaws continued their harassment of the Grants and unremittingly pursued their claim to the lands of Rothiemurchus. To press his claim The Macintosh built a mill just inside the boundary line of their respective properties with the intention of diverting the water from Rothiemurchus to run it. On discovering the plot MacAlpine appealed for assistance from Rob Roy, at the same time sending a peremptory note to The Macintosh to remove the offending mill forthwith. The Macintosh's reply was provocative. He threatened that his intention was to send a force to burn and loot Rothiemurchus, and duly demonstrated his intention by mustering a strong force of men on the march between the two lands. MacAlpine had so far received no response from Rob Roy and fell into a mood of despondency because The Macintosh had a force behind him that MacAlpine could not match. Suddenly, however, Rob Roy walked in, but alone. After the customary courtesies had been dispensed with, MacAlpine asked Rob Roy where his men were, to which Rob Roy replied, "Get your piper to play the MacGregors' Gathering".

No sooner had a few notes droned through the forest than in twos and threes the MacGregors began to appear at Kinrara on the opposite bank of the Spey. Soon there was a fully armed force of one hundred and fifty men on the river bank. When The Macintosh observed such a strong force of the dreaded MacGregors he prudently withdrew his men deep into their own territory. Rob Roy's men and the Rothiemurchus men then proceeded to the mill and burned it to the ground. A letter from Rob Roy to The Macintosh followed, advising him that if he did not desist from harrying MacAlpine the Macintosh lands would be laid waste by fire and sword. A song called the *Muilleann Dubh* (Black Mill) was composed about it and this became one of the finest of reel tunes.

MacAlpine was seventy-eight when his wife died, but still being vigorous and young in spirit he soon contemplated

151

remarrying. A neighbouring proprietor had three daughters and he commanded that each should come in turn and present herself for assessment. The eldest came first, a comely lass and he asked her what she would do with a tocher of gold as high as a mountain. Eagerly she rhapsodised about the clothes and jewels she would buy. Unimpressed, MacAlpine dismissed her and when the second sister came he asked her the same question only to be given the same vapid answer. The youngest and most beautiful on being summoned and the same question being posed to her, answered tactfully that so much gold would be too much of a responsibility for her, and she would therefore give it to her husband. MacAlpine was delighted and promptly married her. History does not tell us if she continued to manipulate the old man throughout their married life.

MacAlpine died in 1743. He was succeeded by his son James who married Lady Jean Gordon, a relation of the Duke of Gordon. She had Jacobite leanings and unknown to her husband secreted and fed a number of the rebels in the grounds of Rothiemurchus.

MacAlpine's widow was unhappy with the new regime at Rothiemurchus and there was constant friction between herself and the new Laird and his wife. One Sunday after church service, at which she had received some sort of slight, she walked over to MacAlpine's grave and taking off a shoe tapped the ground with the heel and cried, "MacAlpine, MacAlpine, rise up for half an hour and see me righted". There is no record that MacAlpine obliged.

One summer about the beginning of the 18th Century Lady Mary Grant, wife of MacAlpine accompanied the women of Rothiemurchus to the summer shielings in *Coire Odhar* (Corrour) at the head of Loch Eanaich. She was pregnant at the time, and it was thought that the change of air, and the peace of the surroundings would benefit her health. And there in a turf bothy she gave birth to her second son, John, who from the circumstances of his birth was named Corrour.

Corrour Grant had a distinguished career in the army and died abroad after long service. The incident of his birth was commemorated by naming a large villa in Rothiemurchus "Corrour". It was here that the present Laird's great grandfather, Sheriff John Peter Grant, and his grandfather Lt. Col. John Peter Grant, Sheriff Substitute, lived for many years.

Traces of the foundations of his birthplace may still be found. He left money to build Coylum Bridge and a house at the head of Loch Eanaich which should always have meal in it. It was said that his successors complied with his wishes for a time keeping not only meal but also a quantity of whisky there. Eventually the practice fell into disuse.

The ancestral home of the Grants of Rothiemurchus was The Doune, a square building in the middle of spacious parks and woodlands on the banks of the Spey. The mansion received its name from a high mound nearby, crowned with trees, which was at one time a dun or fort. The Doune, unoccupied for many years, fell into a state of decay and ruin but now happily it has been restored to its erstwhile elegance.

It was leased for many years by the Duke and Duchess of Bedford. The Duchess was a daughter of the celebrated Jane, Duchess of Gordon, who lived at Kinrara on the opposite bank of the Spey. The Duchess of Bedford appears to have inherited the vivacity and active benevolence of her mother. She entertained many of the leading men of the day including the Lord Chancellor of England, Lord Brougham. When a dispute arose amongst the guests as to whether or not the Lord Chancellor carried the Great Seal with him whenever he travelled the Duchess decided to put the matter to the test immediately. She baked a great cake and marching at the head of her friends to Lord Brougham's bedroom, to which he was confined with a slight fever, she begged him to impress the cake with the Great Seal. He willingly did so and the question was thereupon resolved.

At one time young girls from Rothiemurchus used to trudge through the Lairig Ghru to Braemar each with a basket of eggs on her head to sell there. They must have been surefooted on such rocky terrain, and surely it was a hazardous way of earning a few coppers. One cannot help speculating on the seeming dearth of poultry in the Braemar district, or the lack of demand in Strathspey villages. Possibly, of course, these journeys were made as late as Victorian times when, as a result of Queen Victoria's residence at Balmoral, Deeside became highly popular for summer visitors and the demand for eggs could not be met locally.

Towards the turn of the last century a disastrous fire destroyed a large area of Caledonian Pine on the east shore of the loch. A famous old tree standing on the track called *Rathad nam Meirleach* (The Thieves' Road) was also burned. Along this road came the Lochaber reivers in their forays into Strathspey and Moray and the Laird of Grant of the time, called the Speckled Laird, being a prudent man, tried to procure immunity for his own herds by tying a few bullocks to the tree when the reivers' approach was reported.

To those who have an intimate knowledge and love of the Lands and Forest of Rothiemurchus it is unique in its diversity of interests: there is no other district in the Highlands comparable. It did also have a wealth of folklore but sadly few of the old tales remain. Those that have been recovered are worth preserving and recording.

At the pleasant little meadow of Allt Dhru at the beginning of the Lairig Ghru path one is reminded that this was once a croft tenanted by one of Rob Roy MacGregor's men. Across the river from the ruins of a small building in the meadow the foundations of two fairly large buildings may still be found, and here *Màiri Bhuidhe* (Mairi of the Golden Hair), lived happily with her MacGregor husband. Mairi was a beautiful girl who had bewitching powers over young and old, and also over the very deer. At first the Laird frowned on the marriage, but eventually relented and gave them as a dowry the croft of Allt Dhru, and cattle to stock it. The croft was in the hands of their descendants until 1890 when it became vacant and fell into ruin.

Some of Rob Roy's men remained at Rothiemurchus and became allied with the Laird's household: others married into other families. A tombstone in the Rothiemurchus Churchyard preserves their memory.

A certain bedroom in the Doune of Rothiemurchus was never used by the Grants because no one was able to sleep in it. It seemed to contain an evil spirit. It was, however, fully furnished, and when in fairly recent times the house was rented as a shooting lodge this particular room was assigned to a guest who declared that he would sleep in it undisturbed. The room had an odd shape, but otherwise it was just like any other fully-furnished bedroom.

The guest liked the room and sat by the fire for a while before going to bed, but soon a strange feeling of unease crept over him and a lamp by the window sill seemed to have some hypnotic effect on him. It was one of three paraffin lamps in the room but the other two having been turned off, it began to menace him. He broke into a sweat of fear and rising turned it off. He then went to the door and opened it quietly. A noise from some other quarter of the house made him jump in alarm, and as he turned back into the room a gust of icy wind blew out the stove. In terror he groped for the lamps without success, then tried to reach the door again. The room seemed filled with malignant spirits, and when at last in a panic he found the door he banged his head on the door frame and fell to the floor unconscious.

When he came to he lay on a couch in another room with his head bandaged. His host, alerted by the sound of his fall, hovered over him anxiously to know how he felt, and the reason for his fall. Crestfallen the guest hesitantly recounted all that he remembered about his experience. An old man servant, who had assisted his master in administering to the unfortunate guest, then told him that about two hundred years before the Laird's only son was "*as a chaill*" (deranged), and had been confined to that particular room. On day he had succeeded in freeing himself and had met a servant girl on the stairs whom he had strangled, and then had thrown himself down the stairs to his death.

From the east shore of Loch Gamhain in Rothiemurchus a rough path used to lead up to a small den or cave which became the retreat of a vicious character called Black Sandy. The housekeeper at one of the residences of the Grants of

Rothiemurchus, called The Croft, was a beautiful girl whose charms had besotted the young Laird to such a degree that she had already borne him three or four children. The old Laird was so concerned about his lands possibly being secured by the girl for her children that he called for the assistance of Black Sandy to arrest the wasting of the heritage.

At the time Black Sandy lived in a cottage at the Doune, and served the Laird faithfully despite his evil character. Having the Laird's consent to break the liaison by whatever means he thought best, this vicious character cut off the poor girl's ears. Her friends and relations were so horrified that Sandy, fearing for his life, fled to Grantown. However, during his stay there he almost killed another man and finding that district equally unhealthy he secretly stole back to Rothiemurchus, and took up residence in the wild cat's den. But Rothiemurchus, he realised, was too dangerous for him and he fled to America where, it is claimed, one of his descendants became President of the United States.

The Bodach Cleocain Deirg (The Old Man or Spectre of the Red Cloak) haunted Coylumbridge which used to be called *Cuing Leum* (The Narrow Leap). When he reached manhood, this was bridged by the Laird who was born in a summer shieling in Coire Odhar at the head of Loch Eanaich, Patrick Coire Odhar Grant.

Little is known, for little was recorded about the Bodach's activities. Did he suddenly appear in his scarlet cloak to help the traveller over the chasm, or did he profit from the unfortunates who fell in and were drowned? Was his abode near the famous Medicine Well, a short distance up the road towards Loch Morlich road? You can smell it before you reach it as the atmosphere is permeated with the stench of rotten eggs, and the vegetation all around is discoloured to a yellowish tinge.

Did the ailing people of 'Mar, who tramped the twenty-eight miles through the Lairig Ghru, and others from far and near who came to drink of its healing waters, encounter the Bodach and did he profit from the silver coins they left by way of an offering? The numbers would no doubt include kings and robbers for Glenmore was once a royal forest, and was later a hunting ground for the Barons of Kincardine. Nobody remembers, and no records remain to tell us.

The Medicine Well lies on the South bank of the Luinneag flowing out of Loch Morlich. It is close to the old track leading from Moormore which crosses the present road and the river and leads across the moor to the Lairig Ghru Pass.

The Loch of the Lanky Lad's Son

IN Glen Eanaich only a heap of stones marks the site of Dune's Bothy which stood on a pleasant green on the south bank of the Beannaidh Bheag close to the glen track. *Lochan Mhic Gille Chaoil* (The Loch of the Lanky Lad's Son) lies just over the ridge above the Beannaidh, near its confluence with the Beannaidh Bheag. The derivation of the name is interesting but there are two versions of this old legend.

For many years, up until the time of the 1745 Rebellion, Campbells, MacDonalds and Camerons frequently used the *Rathad nam Meirleach* (the Thieves' Road), to lift the lowlanders' cattle which they regarded as lawful booty. On their return they had few qualms in adding any useful beasts they might spy along the Spey Valley, or in Tulloch or Rothiemurchus.

On one of these forays a band of Camerons lifted a herd from Tulloch while the men were at Forres for mill stones, and only the women, children and aged were at home. Returning home later in the day the Tulloch men learned of their loss, and hastened to Rothiemurchus to enlist aid. This was gladly given, and they set off in hot pursuit. They caught up with the Camerons and a bitter fight was fought. The cattle were recovered and the Camerons routed, but one man either from Tulloch or Rothiemurchus was killed in the affray. He was *Fear na Casan Caol* (the man with the lanky legs) and it was claimed that the Loch was named after him.

A more likely version relates that it was the time of year when the women were living in the summer shielings in Glen Eanaich. On a Sunday they had all gone down to Rothiemurchus to Church leaving the glen deserted except for a herd or bowman on watch. Suddenly he heard the ominous lowing of cattle coming up the glen, and knowing that he was helpless, alone against the reivers, he crept through the heather until he was past the band. He then raced to Rothiemurchus, and burst into the Church raising the alarm. Quickly arming themselves the Rothiemurchus men set off in pursuit but they were outstripped by *MacGille Chaoil* (the lanky fellow's son) who, throwing discretion to the winds, engaged the reivers single-handed until his friends arrived. But his bravery cost him his life, and the Camerons buried his body in a hollow. When the affray ended with the Camerons put to flight, no trace of the body could be found. Some weeks later a Lochaber woman told of his death, and indicated where his body would be found. It was lifted and reburied in the Churchyard at Rothiemurchus.

The tradition may have to some degree been confirmed by the discovery about one hundred years ago of an old dirk near Lochan Mhic Gille Chaoil.

Undiscovered treasure may lie hidden somewhere in Rothiemurchus. MacGillie Chaoil was apparently a cautious fellow, and buried his money and valuables in a corner known only to himself. It is said that if by chance anyone wandering the forest sees a white serpent entering a hole there assuredly will he find the hoard of the lanky fellow's son. To see a white serpent was at one time regarded as an omen of good fortune to come.

Before reaching the Beannaidh Bheag there are two knolls close by the Beannaidh called *Toman na da Mhurchadh* (The Knoll of the Two Murdochs). Here, tradition claims, was witnessed one of the last scenes of primitive justice, ordeal by combat. Each Murdoch had a knoll to himself, and each had a bow and a quiver full of arrows. After a good deal of skirmishing for advantage one of the contestants would be pierced by an arrow and honour satisfied.

The Old Man and the Old Woman

THE sentinels of Glen Eanaich are two pillars of rock rising high above Loch Eanaich, *Am Bodach* (The Old Man) and *A' Chailleach* (The Old Woman). *Am Bodach*, a squat figure on the skyline as you work westwards round the ridge north of Loch nan Cnapan is a striking contrast to the tall, austere figure of *A' Chailleach* standing a little way down the cliffs of *Sgor Gaoith* (The Windy Peak) on the edge of Coire na Cailleach.

There was a time when the local people believed that these turbulent characters resented mortals entering their domain at certain times, but such was the enmity between them that if the one were wrathful with the intruder the other would encourage him with friendly cries. A cold woman, *A' Chailleach*, especially in the spring when on account of being in shade she retains her white mantle longer than *Am Bodach* who sits benignly in full sun. It was said that when storm broke out and thunder and lightening echoed and flashed around the high tops *Am Bodach* and *A' Chailleach* must be having a right royal battle.

There are a number of rocky outcrops in the Highlands bearing the name *Bodach* or *Cailleach*. The formation of Loch Ness, many islands, the fullness of corn wrack were all attributed to the *Cailleach*. She was hardly the sunny Ceres of the South but a capricious Goddess at whose behest the seas boiled and the winds screamed over the mountain tops where she lived. Perhaps the Glen Eanaich Cailleach is the same mythical person as *Cailleach Bheur* (the old woman or witch of the pinnacle) who has given her name to a number of places in the West Highlands. Traditionally the *Cailleach Bheur* immersed herself every one hundred years in the water of Loch Ba, on the Isle of Mull, in order to rejuvenate herself. This had to be done before dawn because if a cock crowed, or a dog barked the charm became useless. One morning she cut it too fine and as she was about to take the plunge a dog barked and the *Cailleach* fell down dead.

Another story about the Cailleach Bheur is that she was so gigantic that she could wade the Sound of Mull knee deep.

> *Cur-lochan dubh, dorcha, domhain,*
> *Aon Loch as coimhne 'san domhan;*
> *Cha ruigeadh Caol Muile ach mo ghluinean*
> *Ach ruigeadh Loch Crulaich mo shleistean*

> Cur-lochan black, dark, deep
> A loch m'all conscience deep.
> The Sound of Mull will reach only to my knees
> But Loch Crulaich will reach to my thighs.

Every morning it is said that she drove her favourite cow from the Mull of Kintyre to the summit of Ben Cruachan, a distance of about eighty miles, so that it could drink from a favourite well and increase its milk supply. She pastured her herds of deer, they said, on the waters that lie between the Torran Rocks on Mull and Dubh Hirteach, twenty miles out into the Atlantic.

Perhaps the *Cailleach* of Glen Eanaich sometimes waded knee deep across the loch to attempt to intimidate the Old Man.

Big Donald, King of the Fairies

Domhnull Mór Bad an t-Sithean, or Big Donald, King of the Fairies in Glenmore, was by all accounts of immense stature. His home was the two little knolls one hundred feet or so in height a little to the West of Loch Morlich called the *Sithean*, or Fairy Knolls. He was not always popular because he played many a prank on the glen people.

But once he did them a good turn. Before the introduction of paraffin oil homes were lit with torch fir, and certain people from the Lowlands had the privilege of gathering this material from the forest. They stayed with the crofters, and grazed their horses on their land. They were a nuisance, and the natives wished to be rid of them. *Domhnull Mór* heard of their troubles and resolved to rid the glen of these unwelcome visitors.

One day when the visitors were gathering the torch fir they were startled to see a gigantic figure who instantly attacked them with sticks and stones, and panicked them into fleeing the glen. It is believed that they never returned.

Another time Robin Òg Stewart of Kincardine was on his way home when he met a band of *Domhnull*'s clan on the march with pipers at their head. Their pipes were bejewelled, and their drones were of silver. Entranced with the beauty of the spectacle and the music he threw his bonnet among them crying, "Mine to you, yours to me", and snatched one of the pipes. The pipers marched on apparently unaware of the uncouth antics of a mere mortal, their music sounding sweeter and merrier than before. Robin, full of glee, hid his prize beneath his plaid and hurried home, only to find that the precious bagpipes had turned into a broken blade of grass and an empty puff ball.

At *Lochan Uaine* (Green Loch) in the Pass of Revoan it is so still when all is quiet that our thoughts sometimes dwell on our rude forefathers, and the sound of the ancient Barons of Kincardine's hunting horns. It is tempting to believe that you can hear the elfin maidens singing '*Crodh Chailean*' as they milk the hinds, or glimpse *Domhnull Mór* himself with his elfin band sailing their skiffs or holding revels on a stretch of green sward, as the pipers play gay tunes.

The loch is fed from an underground spring or springs and the relics of ancient trees lie in its depths. But why is the water as green as the Atlantic? The answer is very simple of course. For was it not here that *Domhnull Mór* and his fairy band washed their clothes? Scientists will discourse learnedly about matter in suspension being the cause but who wants to listen?

Near *Lochan Uaine* are the ruins of a shieling called *Ruigh da Ros* (Shieling of the two Points or Promontories). Towards the end of the last century a man called Seumas Robertson lived here all alone. He was an Army pensioner, a hard, surly fellow who seemed to have an unreasonable hatred of women. He had, however, a charm for healing eye afflictions. On one occasion a woman of the name of Elizabeth MacQueen timidly knocked at his door and was harshly commanded to enter. When Seumas looked up from mending his brogan and saw his visitor was a woman has asked in a fury, "What do you want here?" When the poor, trembling woman told him about the trouble she was having with her eyes he sneered, "I'll give you an *obaidh* (charm) that you won't forget —

> *Na faiceadh do shuil go brath*
> *'N darna te na sgladhair odhar*
> *An te eile na sgleodhair bhan*

> If you had your eyes for ever
> The second one would be grey
> The other one a white mass.

Terrified by the prediction that her sight would be lost forever the poor woman rushed from the cottage and tradition says that she never recovered her sight. From then on she was known as *Ealasaid Cham* (Blind Elsie) to the end of her days.

163

Near *Lochan Uaine* there are two unnamed holes. These were used by the Glenmore people to ambush Lochaber raiders as they passed west with their plunder from the low country.

In the vicinity are several wells. One was very deep, almost sixteen feet. It was named *Fuaran Ghamhainn* (Stirk's Well) because a stirk fell into it and drowned.

To the east of the loch lies *Fuaran Nam Poit*. It received its name because it was close to the bog where the summer shieling pots were buried in Autumn when the people returned home to their crofts for the winter and spring months.

The Spectre of the Bloody Hand

AT the east end of Loch Morlich the thickets near the golden sands were at one time the home of the *Bodach Lamh Dheirg* (Old Man or Spectre of the Bloody Hand). He was a gigantic figure, it seems, clad in the full panoply of a highland warrior. One hand was always dripping with blood: perhaps in his mortal life it had been badly injured in some affray. To anyone unfortunate enough to meet him there was an instant challenge to mortal combat. If the challenge was accepted boldly no harm followed but to the timorous, insufficiently versed in the art of mediæval repartee, and averse to sword play there were dire consequences. Despite his terrifying appearance and bellicose attitude there appears to have been a kind and humane streak in him, for he assumed the role of guardian of the deer and other wild creatures in the forest, and woe betide any hunter who trespassed too much in his domain.

Robin Òg Stewart of Kincardine was one day hunting in Glenmore, and succeeded in bringing down a fat young hind with a well-aimed arrow. He proceeded to gralloch the beast, and for a moment laid his *sgian dubh* on the grass, but on bending down to pick it up again he discovered that it had disappeared. Thinking little of that because it could well have just slipped out of sight under the hind, he drew the knife from the scabbard of his dirk only to find that when he laid it down it also disappeared. By this time he had become perplexed and uneasy, and finishing his work as quickly as possible set off for Kincardine at a trot with the young hind over his shoulders.

Some time elapsed before he returned to Glenmore but this time on the shores of Loch Morlich he met an old man in a grey plaid.

"*Sin thu fhein Robin Òg*" (It is yourself young Robin) he said, and pointing a bloody finger at Robin he continued, "You are too often in the Glen slaughtering my poor innocents. You killed a hind not long ago in *Glac an beallaidh* (Hollow of the Broom), as you call it, I call it *Glac an beadaidh* (Hollow of the Impudence). Here are your knives, but have a care for the future."

The warning was enough for Robin Og, and thereafter he changed his hunting ground.

In Macfarlane's *Geographical Collections* Vol. III there is a quaint reference to *Lamh Dheirg*:

"Kairne Gorum, a famous hill, which is four miles high: Gold hath been found here. The Hill aboundeth with excellent Crystall. There is much telling of a spirit called Ly Erg that frequents the Glenmore. He appears with a red hand in the habit of a soldier and challenges men to fight with him as lately in 69 he fought with three Brothers one after another who immediately died thereafter."

Now none need have any fears providing they do not poach the deer and leave wounded animals to die a slow and painful death on the hills. With such it seems he can be as ruthless as ever. "*Thoir an aire!*" (beware unskilful sportsmen and careless poachers).

Sir Walter Scott had this to say about the *bochdan*:

"The Forest of Glenmore, in the North Highlands, is believed to be haunted by a spirit called LHAM-DEARG, in the array of an ancient warrior having a bloody hand, from which he takes his name. He insists upon those with whom he meets doing battle with him; and the clergyman who makes up an account of the district, extant in the MacFarlane M.S., circa 1670, in the Advocates Library, gravely assures us that in his time Lhamh-Dearg fought with three brothers whom he met in his walk, none of whom long survived the bloody conflict."

Sir Walter's spelling of the bodach's name is a little astray. However, he again refers to the *Bodach Lamh Dheirg* in *Marmion*:

And such a phantom too, 'tis said

166

With Highland broadsword, targe and plaid,
And fingers, red with gore
Is seen in Rothiemurchus glade.

The Tailors' Stone

THE Tailors' Stone is a massive table of rock which lies beside the track in the Pass of Lairig Ghru, a short distance west of the burn the flows from Coire nan Taillearan on Ben Mac Dhui.

In olden days the tailors of Abernethy in Strathspey seem to have had a reputation for boastfulness, especially when under the influence of John Barleycorn. One Hogmanay three of them in their cups boasted that they would dance at the dells of Abernethy, Rothiemurchus and Braemar within twenty-four hours. They danced at Nethy, and they danced at Rothiemurchus; then bold with the spirit of their boast, and the spirit of friend John B. they set off for the airy heights of the Lairig Ghru. Past the shieling of Allt Dhru they trudged, roaring and singing lustfully. The softer ground near the tree line sobered them a little but they strode on, unsteadily but manfully, as only Abernethy tailors might. They reached the summit of the Pass but on the descent to the Mar side a sudden blizzard blew up. They struggled on as far as the stone which bears their name and here they lay down in the lee of the boulder to shelter from the storm. Utterly fatigued they fell asleep, and died where they lay.

There is also a tailor's stone on Cairngorm, so called in memory of Seamus, a local tailor who was an enthusiastic poacher. In the rutting season when the 'Mar stags were in the habit of crossing to Glenmore to seek the hinds, he took his cloth and rifle to the hill, where he sat cross-legged on the stone, working steadily but all the time keeping a sharp look-out for any suitable stag that might come within range.

The Argyll Stone

TWO tales are told to account for the name of this prominent stone on the ridge on the west side of Glen Eanaich. The first tells that in the year 1594, during the reign of King James VI, the Duke of Argyll was despatched with a large force to suppress an alleged rising led by the Earls of Huntly and Errol who were trying to restore Roman Catholicism as the recognised religion. His orders were to quell the rising and apprehend Huntly and Errol, but in both objects he failed ingloriously. He was routed at the Battle of Allt na Coilleachan in Glenlivet and compelled to make a hurried withdrawal southwards. Tradition says that he rested his men and allowed them to snatch a hasty meal beside the stone on the lower shoulders of Sgoran Dubh. Hence the name, Argyll Stone.

The second version claims that in 1642-43 Argyll pursued Montrose northwards from Blair Atholl. The route taken was through Glen Bruar to the head of Glen Feshie, thence along the ridges to the point where the huge stone stands. From here he descended to the low ground, passed through Rothiemurchus and defeated Montrose at the East end of Alvie Moor. Montrose escaped with his bodyguard and fled through Badenoch towards Fort Augustus. Within perhaps the last fifty years several pieces of armour were found on the battlefield and retrained by the finder, Captain Cumming of Putney.

The Big Grey Man

THE "biography" of the Big Grey Man was published under the title *The Big Grey Man of Ben Macdhui* by the author in 1970. This is a study in depth of a phenomenon which has never been fully explained. In this chapter it will suffice to recount the legend briefly.

The legendary Big Grey Man of Ben Macdhui has been a controversial subject for the past fifty years during which a volume of correspondence has appeared in the press describing and questioning the strange, and often frightening experiences of climbers on Ben Macdhui. Innumerable articles have appeared in both press and magazines, and the subject has been discussed a number of times on radio and television. Passing reference is made to the phenomenon in a number of books, and whole chapters are devoted to it. As far back as the early 19th Century James Hogg, the Ettrick Shepherd (1770-1835) in verse, and John Hill Burton in his *The Cairngorm Mountains* (1854) gave credence to the Grey Man. Recently, as a result of painstaking research, a formidable mass of evidence on the subject was recorded.

Stories about the Grey Man are legion, but when subjected to investigation and analysis a large proportion of them proved to be manifestly absurd fabrications, or, with the writer's eye on his public, richly embellished old stories which, in their original form, were experiences recounted by people who sincerely believed that they had encountered something of abnormal proportions on Ben Macdhui.

In a brief article it is impossible to present a list of the more credible stories which have been recorded, but the two which follow will reveal some of the difficulties inherent in the

170

problem for they emanate from men of the highest integrity, and of vast experience of mountains world-wide.

The classic and most credible story of stark terror on Ben Macdhui is, of course, the experience of the late Professor Norman Collie which dates back to 1891, but which he did not publicly reveal in this country for another thirty-four years. He had, however, told the story in New Zealand at a much earlier date.

Collie was a native of Aberdeenshire, and became the first Professor of Organic Chemistry at the University of London (1902-1928). He was regarded as one of the greatest climbers of his generation, his experience ranging from the Himalayas to the Caucasus, and the Alps to the Rockies. But he did not ignore the lesser peaks of home and the Skye Cuillin was his favourite climbing ground. Indeed *Sgurr Thormaid* is named after him.

He was accustomed to loneliness on mountains, but he confessed at the Annual General Meeting and Dinner of the Cairngorm Club in November 1925, that he had experienced the most intense fear of his lifetime when climbing alone on Ben Macdhui:

"I was returning from the cairn on the summit in a mist when I began to think I heard something else than merely the noise of my own footsteps. For every few steps I took I heard a crunch, and then another crunch as if someone was walking after me but taking steps three or four times the length of my own.

I said to myself, 'This is all nonsense'. I listened and heard it again, but could see nothing in the mist. As I walked on and the eerie crunch, crunch, sounded behind me I was seized with terror and took to my heels, staggering blindly among the boulders for four or five miles nearly down to Rothiemurchus Forest.

Whatever you make of it I do not know, but there is something very queer about the top of Ben MacDhui and I will not go back there again by myself I know."

The story has been repeated so often that over the years it has been badly distorted to a degree which would have dismayed the austere Professor. It has been claimed by some that Collie asserted he saw a huge grey figure, but it may be accepted as irrefutable that the experience as narrated that evening was circumscribed by sounds only, and the sense of something inimical near to him.

When the story hit the headlines it was greeted with some scepticism, and numerous facile explanations were put forward in the crop of letters to the press which followed: the Spectre of the Brocken, falling stones, wind in the gullies, the movement of deer; but these explanations were not acceptable to everyone. The sceptics scornfully maintained that Collie's 'yarn' was the result of after-dinner euphoria and nothing more, while others who knew the man intimately condemned this as gross vilification of his character, and pointed out that a study of his career and ascetic personality must convince the most ardent sceptic of his utter sincerity, whether the story was judged to be the result of hallucination or otherwise.

The news of Collie's experience eventually reached the ears of Dr. A.M. Kellas, another famous mountaineer who carried out much pioneer work in the Himalayas, and who died in Tibet and was buried within sight of Everest while taking part in the 1921-22 first Mount Everest (Reconnaissance) Expedition. He wrote to Collie claiming that he had actually seen the Grey Man while he and his brother were chipping for crystals in a hollow below the summit of the Ben. Suddenly, they saw a giant figure coming down towards them from the cairn. It passed out of sight in a dip, but while awaiting its reappearance fear possessed them, and they fled down *Coire Etchachan* obsessed with the urge to get away from the mountain and the "Thing" that followed at their heels. There was a mist on part of the hill that day, but they refused to believe that the figure could have been the shadow of either of them causing an optical illusion. If that had been the case why not two shadows?

Some of the explanations put forward to explain Collie's fear might well have been responsible in both these cases, but if so it seems odd that two men of such wide experience as Collie and Kellas should have been thus fooled; and it is unthinkable that either, or both, would have subscribed to a leg-pull in such peculiar taste. Both experiences may indeed by capable of a perfectly natural explanation, but if so it is strange that neither of these men, both with highly trained scientific minds, could find a logical explanation of the uncanny 'something' which they sensed, which caused fear to seize them by the throat and urged them from the mountain. It is, perhaps, significant that neither felt any shame in confessing that he had fled from it ignominiously.

Ghostly voices and music, and strange, enormous bilobular footprints which have never been identified play an important part in a study of the Grey Man phenomenon. Talking, laughing and chanting have been distinctly heard, and sounds of music of a beautiful sweetness of timbre rising and falling from a whisper to a full and rounded crescendo, then to a final dying cadence in diminuendo, outburst of melody as if a door were opening and shutting upon a room. Treble and bass voices were often distinguishable, accompanied and enriched throughout by instrumental music. Basically, such sounds are accounted for by the rise and fall of the wind funnelling through crevices in the rocks, the rush of water, the movement of underlying scree and one's own heightened imagination, for similar sounds may be heard in open, grassy corries devoid of wind, water or rocks. But to some these sounds are inaudible.

The grey image which has so frequently been observed in the Cairngorms has sometimes been postulated as the only logical explanation of the Big Grey Man. This phenomenon is, however, a very simple one which was first observed on the Brocken, the highest summit of the Hartz Mountains in Germany, and became familiar as 'The Spectre of the Brocken'. It is simply the shadow of the observer thrown by a low sun against an opaque wall of mist. The result is that the shadow is magnified enormously, and is sometimes distorted to the most grotesque forms depending on wind currents and the observer's own movements. Occasionally the shadow is surrounded by beautiful bows of bright prismatic colours, sometimes called 'the glory', which, under these circumstances, is simply the chromatic fringe developed by diffraction at the

173

margin of the dark shadow. The spectacle is startling until the observer becomes aware that he is simply looking at his own image.

Perhaps inevitably the phenomenon has been linked with unidentified flying objects, and such like. It seems ludicrous to even suggest that Ben Macdhui may be an earth fall for visitors from outer space, but, however improbable, the claim had been made with the deepest conviction in certain quarters, notably the Aetherius Society, in whose words the Ben is a 'centre of cosmic intelligence': in fact, the home and laboratory internally of spacemen: 'The Great White Brotherhood'.

Linked but not necessarily associated with the claims of the Aetherius Society are those of the Buddhist and allied religions, chiefly the Countess of Mayo's Active Truth Academy. The belief is resolutely held by some of the followers that Ben Macdhui is the haunt of a particularly 'holy' or 'perfect' being, and that levitated Tibetan lamas regularly meet there to discuss the destinies of the world. In 1960 the Countess declared to a press correspondent that she was to have held a rendezvous with them in a cave on the Ben, but on account of bad weather it had been postponed.

Captain Sir Hugh Rankin, Bart., a practising Mahayana Buddhist who was vice-President of the World Buddhist Association in 1945, and the second British person to perform the Holy Buddhist Pilgrimage in 1944, described in the press on two occasions an actual encounter with the Big Grey Man in the Lairig Ghru pass. He was instantly recognised as a Bodhisattva, one of the five 'Perfected Men' of the Buddhist faith who control the destinies of the world, and who meet once a year in a cave in the Himalayas. He was an enormous, benign being who spoke in a language which neither Sir Hugh nor Lady Rankin could understand, but they were undismayed by his presence and, bowing to him, Sir Hugh said in Urdu, "I bow to the Lord Bodhisattva who rules the destinies of the world". He stayed with them for about ten minutes during which a heavenly host of musicians played high up in the sky. Then he was gone.

The story provoked the following poem from Lilian Duncan Robb, Aberdeen:

If ever ye gang through the Lairig Ghru-
(Abominable Snowman's there the noo!)
Dinna produce a Hielan cromach-
Or try to poke him in the stomach.
For he is 'fifty' round the chest
And wears a lang robe for a vest.
So if ye hike through Lairig Ghru,
(Grasping claymore and skean dubh),
Gie him a greeting, like Sir Hugh,
But try the Gaelic, nae Urdu.

Are all these tales of weird experiences on Ben Macdhui capable of explanation by natural means, or does some supernatural influence invest the high plateau and environs of the mountain?

Without a doubt many are the result of misinterpretation of perfectly natural phenomena, and some are clearly the result of hysteria or self-induced hypnosis in minds absorbed with stories of the Grey Man, and aggravated by agoraphobia, fatigue, debility or morbid sensitivity; in other words it would appear that some of the narrators experienced exactly what they wished to experience, or had become a prey to uncontrollable imagination.

Loneliness in remote places engenders so many opportunities for the imagination to play fast and loose with rationalism. In the gathering gloom of night particularly, or the breaking dawn when dark, primeval faces seem to stare down from the cliffs, and grey, amorphous shadows flit from rock to rock hearing sharpens to sounds which momentarily rise above the pentatonic dirge of the wind, and the ears may become sharp as a wild animal's with fear. It is then conceivably when confronted with the intangible and incomprehensible, that fear is triggered off and an insensate dread of the unknown takes possession. Self-hypnosis quickened by the inheritance of age-old dreads could do the rest, and the only refuge-flight from the mountain. Perhaps after all only an alter ego dogging the footsteps!

Some of the stories are fundamentally psychic in origin, and even although psychic phenomena are so often attributed to the activities of the subconscious they still do not escape from the actual. They cannot therefore be impatiently discarded as emanating from abnormal brains.

It must be conceded that there is testimony which cannot be ignored, and if we discard all the palpable falsehoods, and in all probability a welter of optical illusions, hoaxes, hallucinations and imperfect observations a hard core of mystery seems to remain, unsolved and challenging.

William Smith of Rynuie

WILLIAM Rynuie, as he was commonly known, was a native of the Parish of Abernethy. He was a man of bold and resolute character with a powerful physique, capable of enduring any amount of fatigue and exposure. He was a renowned deer stalker and professional poacher who, with the connivance of the Laird of Rothiemurchus made a practice of raiding the Forest of Mar. His stalking bothy was at the foot of Derry Cairngorm, and the "fail" foundation in a sheltered nook of the stream that runs out of Lochan Uaine may still be found by searching closely.

Legend has it that he perished in an avalanche in the *Garbh Choire Mor of Braeriach*. In actual fact he was finally compelled to abandon his lawless way of life and joined the Army. He served under Sir John Moor, and died at Portsmouth shortly after the disastrous retreat from Corunna.

He was a nature lover, philosopher and poet — indeed he was sometimes called the Cairngorm Poet — and his songs breathe the essence of poetry. The composition of "*Aig Allt an Lochan Uaine*" (By the Stream of the Green Loch) is particularly beautiful, and was declared faultless by the most competent critics of the time. It is the Stalker's Dream —

> Aig Allt an Lochan Uaine
> Bha miuair a' tamh,
> Ged bha an t-aite fuar
> Bha'n fhardach fuasach blath.
> Ged thigeadh gaoth 'o thuath orm
> 'Us cathadh luath o'n aird,
> Bha Allt an Lochan Uaine,
> Le' fhuaim ga m'chuir gu pramh.

(By the stream of the Green Loch I once had my lonely dwelling and although the situation was cold the interior was remarkably warm, and although the piercing north wind often blew the drifting snow from the high tops the gurgling of the frozen stream soothed my weary eyes to sleep.)

There was a tradition handed down in the family of the Mackenzies of Whitewell which had been resident in Rothiemurchus for generations that the Big Grey Man of Ben MacDhui was the ghost of an ancestor who said in one of his poems that he would "come again". To her dying day the late Carrie Mackenzie (Mrs. Nethersole-Thompson) was unshakeable in her conviction that the ghost of her ancestor, *Uilleam Ruighe Naoimhe*, haunted the Ben MacDhui plateau.

The Old Woman of the Stones

ABOUT one hundred and sixty years ago an old Banffshire widow was to be found exploring every burn and corrie in the Cairngorms in search of the valuable Cairngorm stone she had for so long dreamed of finding. Perhaps she had heard of a wonderful stone that had been glinting in the moonlight from a seemingly unscalable cliff rising from Loch A'an. Year after year she returned each summer, and spent many days and nights sleeping out rough in whatever shelter she could find. No doubt the celebrated Shelter Stone at the head of Loch A'an was one of her temporary abodes. She became so well known to the local people that she became known as *A'Chailleach nan Cloiche* (the Old Woman of the Stones):

> Time pass'd on while still her lonely efforts found
> No recompense, derided and at length
> Pitied by many as insane of mind.

But she disregarded what people thought or said, and at long last her diligence was rewarded. She found a beautiful beryl which is a much rarer stone than the Cairngorm stone. It was about the size of a wine glass and of great beauty. Through the good offices of the Parish Minister a purchaser was found, and to her great joy the widow's purse was filled.

Once a gentleman of high degree encountered her in Glen A'an, and asked her is she was not sometimes afraid in such wild places alone. "Why should I be afraid?" she asked, "I never see anyone worse than myself, and God is as near me here as in the plains." Her diligence was again rewarded, and she found many more Cairngorms. The biggest and best was purchased by the Laird of Invercauld, and it may well be that the stone on view in Braemar Castle from May to October is the self-same stone. It weighs about fifty-two pounds, and measures approximately fifteen inches long by five inches deep. The colour is a mixture of black and yellowish gold and it is believed that it was found on Ben A'an.

Another diligent searcher for Cairngorms was "Old Revoan", James Grant of Revoan. He found a stone beside the *Feith Buidhe* on the Cairngorm-Ben MacDhuie plateau which weighed about 50 lbs. It was purchased by Queen Victoria for the sum of £50.

Another was Charles Robertson, who, for a number of years, was watcher at the Corrour Bothy. On one occasion, when King Edward VIII was taking part in a deer drive in Glen Giusachan, Charlie was too occupied to do more than hastily mark some fine crystals appearing through the sand at the side of a little burn on *Monadh Mór*. Disappointingly, when he returned a few days later they were nowhere to be seen.

Searching for Cairngorms was in fact quite a small industry at one time, and some of the holes or pots where the searchers worked may still be encountered. As to their commercial value this does not amount to a great deal unless a really fine specimen is discovered.

In the Old Statistical Account of Scotland published in 1795 reference is made to the crystals found on the Cairngorms:

"On them are found pellucid stones, of the nature of precious stones, equally transparent, beautiful in their colour: and some of them, particularly the emerald, as hard as any oriental gem of the same kind. The most common are, the brown, of different shades, and next the topaz. There are also beautiful amethysts and emeralds, though these are rare to be met with, particularly the latter; and what is remarkable, amethysts are only to be found on Loch-na-Garaich (Lochnagar); emeralds and topazes, and the brown only on Binn-na muick-duidhe (Ben MacDhui) and the other mountains in these parishes. The first of these stones that attracted notice, and were cut by a lapidary, were found on Cairngorm in Strathspey, but connected with the above ridge of mountains, which gave rise, though very improperly, to the general name of Cairn-gorm stones."

Tragedy of the Abernethy Soldiers

IN December 1804 a party of Abernethy soldiers set off on leave from their barracks in Edinburgh to walk home. In due course they reached Braemar and rested the night. Despite warnings of the dangers that might lie ahead in view of the threatening weather, they refused to be dissuaded from continuing their journey the next day. Amply provided for with food from the good people of Braemar they set off again. They reached the Derry, and pressed on up Glen Derry despite the gathering storm clouds. Before they reached the head of the glen snow began to fall, and at *Lochan a' Bhainne* the drift was so severe that they lost their bearings, and instead of veering west and breasting the easy slope of the *Lairig an Laoigh* they followed the rough course of the Glas Allt. Here they floundered in deep snow and choking spindrift, became separated and gradually so fatigued that one by one they lay down and died, until only three of the party remained alive.

Donald Elder and two brothers, Alexander and William Forsyth, pushed on valiantly, and when Alexander collapsed William took him on his back. In turn William collapsed and died, and only Donald Elder and Alexander Forsyth reached Abernethy to tell the tragic tale.

The other comrades who perished were John Tulloch, Donald Cameron, Donald Ross and Peter Mackenzie. The body of John Tulloch was found in a peat hag at Ruigh Allt an Fheidh, near the junction of the Glas Allt and Uisge Dubh Poll a' Choin. Peter Mackenzie came by Carn Tarsuinn, and his body was not recovered for about eighteen months. Cameron of Culachy was on the hills at the time looking for a strayed horse when he spied something white in the distance. Thinking it was the carcase of his horse he approached and found the ghastly remains of Mackenzie. The flesh was torn and the head severed from the neck.

MacCallum the Poacher

UPPER Strathspey was notable for its poachers. They were clean in their methods; ethical according to their lights, and they displayed no vicious traits towards those who so assiduously tried to bring them to book except one: Alan MacCallum of Tulloch whose exploits were so outrageous that he became a much wanted man.

On December 20th 1890 he was staying in a hovel at Milton of Tulloch when two constables, Thomas King, Nethy Bridge, and John MacNiven, Boat of Garten, arrived to arrest him for non-payment of a fine imposed for poaching. The fine amounted to 5/- plus £2:17:0d. for expenses. As they approached the cottage MacCallum moved out to a wood nearby, and when the constables eventually located him he had a gun in his hand. He pointed it at P.C. MacNiven, and told him that he would shoot him through the heart if he interfered with his liberty. The Constables prudently retired, but at dusk, when they felt assured that MacCallum was again inside the two-roomed cottage, they decided to tackle him again.

P.C. MacNiven entered a dark bedroom where he was attacked by a dog. It yelped when he hit it hard on the head with his truncheon, and immediately a loud report came from the other room. "Are you alright King?", MacNiven shouted, but he received no reply. Groping his way through to the other room MacNiven stumbled over something behind the door, and, striking a match, he was horrified to find his colleague murdered. Across his legs lay MacCallum's single barrelled muzzle-loading gun. It had just been fired for it was still warm, but there was no trace of the murderer.

The alarm was raised, and it was reported to the police that MacCallum had been seen at the time of the murder running from the house barefooted, but carrying another gun. It was discovered that he had made for the house of John Stewart, an old man who lived about a mile west of MacCallum's house.

"Could you give me a pair of boots John?" he asked.

"Yes", said John, "I have a pair here, but they are gey hard."

"I will soon soften them in the burn", said MacCallum.

Reinforcements were rushed to the district, and the hunt for the wanted man was on. It was three days, however, on the evening of 23rd December, before MacCallum was captured at the farm of Tomachrochar on the west side of Nethy Bridge, where he had sought refuge. He was in a state of exhaustion, and covered in mud. He made no attempt to resist, and begged a glass of milk, a piece, and a lie-down in the barn. He was given a glass of whisky and milk, and some food to revive him before being moved to Inverness jail.

He appeared at the Inverness sitting of the High Court on February 14th 1899, and arraigned on the charge of threatening to kill P.C. MacNiven, and of murdering P.C. King, but before the trial commenced intimation was made of a special defence that when the crime was committed the prisoner was not sane.

The Judge gave vent to the prevailing feeling of sympathy for the wretched poacher by remarking, "Could this haggard, downcast creature be the once daring and successful raider of deer preserves, the man of iron will who dwelt in the fastnesses of the forest, ranging it by day and by night defying, and for long eluding gamekeepers and police and living on the proceeds of his lawless activities and woodcraft skills?"

Witnesses for the defence were called, and three medical men testified that although his behaviour on a number of occasions created doubts about his sanity they did not have reason to believe that he was a lunatic. A number of MacCallum's acquaintances testified that he frequently complained of headaches which MacCallum himself believed was the result of having suffered from sunstroke when he was a shepherd in Patagonia. Lord Traynor in his address to the jury reminded them that there was no evidence to show that MacCallum was insane when he committed the crime. They should, however, consider that because of the approach of the police to arrest him, and the arousal this caused might have led the accused to become not fully responsible for the moment. If they thought the crime had been committed in blind rage the law afforded no protection.

The verdict was held guilty by unanimous voice on the charge of threatening Constable MacNiven, and by a majority found guilty of culpable homicide on the second charge. "The jury have taken a very merciful view of the case", the Judge remarked, and sentenced MacCallum to fifteen years penal servitude. MacCallum apparently remained quite composed throughout the proceedings, except once when a witness declared that the accused confessed to hearing voices telling him that he would suffer on earth for his sins. In a loud voice MacCallum cried, "No, no".

Perhaps McCallum's mind had been unhinged to some extent for years. He had a bitter hatred of the Game Laws, and he became reckless of any consequences in his anxiety to retain his liberty. He had always been a dare-devil cateran roaming the hills, and glens and taking what he felt was his right.

He fell in love with a local girl, but then he was jilted. Disillusioned, he became gloomy and sullen. In 1887 he disappeared from Tulloch. Later it was learned that he had gone to Patagonia where he became a ranch shepherd. Four years later he returned to Tulloch more dour, surly, and unsociable than ever. He secured a job as a gamekeeper at Roschall in the Black Isle, but he terrorised people in the district by locking himself in a house, refusing food and entrance to anyone. He started to fire off guns in the house, and naturally such behaviour earned him his dismissal.

He then became wholly antisocial and lived a lone wolf life in the woods of Abernethy. A poem entitled "MacCallum's Lament" was written following his arrest in December 1898.

Farewell to the hills and the dells of Strathspey,

To the green woods of Tulloch oh farewell for aye,
To Nethy's sweet murmur I'll listen no more,
Nor roam the dark forest of gloomy Glenmore.

Farewell to the grouse, to the roe and the deer,
They may now roam in pleasure MacCallum's not here,
For hunting them surely I've had my fair share,
The keepers that knew me approached me with care.

So when two daring Bluecoats my house did assail,
For to frighten me off words were of no avail.
In an unguarded moment brave King I shot dead,
I was always a believer in powder and lead.

Bad luck to the man who first handed me o'er,
To be chained like a dog and remembered no more.
A curse on all keepers, the Police and all,
They accompanied my ruin, they hastened my fall.

The scenes of my childhood I'll ne'er see again,
The prayers of my parents they were all in vain.
Dark, dark was the night I first handled a gun,
The powers of hell had already begun.

To all you young poachers take a warning from me,
Lay aside all your guns whilst you're able and free,
And enjoy life's sweet blessings and work for your bread,
And remember MacCallum long after he's dead.

Another poem, entitled "The Murder of Constable King",
by an anonymous rhymester, was published on 20th December
1898. It rambles on for twenty-six verses and can hardly be
described as a classic.

MacCallum served his full sentence at Peterhead. It is
reported that while there he gave considerable trouble to the
Governor and his staff. Little appears to be known of his life
after he emerged from prison. It is commonly believed that he
emigrated to Canada and never returned. The late Gillies
Lobban, an old friend of the Author, who was born and bred
at Kincardine, and whose knowledge of the tales of the district
was encyclopaedic, was firmly of the belief that MacCallum
spent his remaining years in a Salvation Army Home in
Glasgow. A recent enquiry to the Salvation Army Headquarters

in Glasgow discovered no information about him. A similar enquiry to the Governor of H.M. Prison, Peterhead, revealed that the records there do not go as far back as 1899. The Scottish Home & Health Department was equally unfruitful. All the relevant prison records up to 1914 which are held by the Scottish Records Office were closely examined by Miss M.L. Aitken of the Scottish Home & Health Department, but they contain no reference to MacCallum.

Constable King was buried in Abernethy Churchyard (i.e. Abernethy in Strathspey) and the headstone above the grave was erected by the Inverness-shire Constabulary.

This chapter in Strathspey history was recalled on Friday 15th April 1977 when the ashes of the late Thomas King, a son of the murdered Constable, were buried next to his father's grave. Sixty-eight years after that fateful night of murder a man called on Chief Inspector Andrew McClure, later Depute Chief Constable, and introduced himself as the dead Constable's son. He told Mr. McClure that he had emigrated to Australia as a young man of nineteen, and expressed a wish that when he died his ashes would be sent back to this country, and buried beside his father's grave. From that time Mr. McClure and James MacIntyre, who was then Chief Constable, kept in touch with him. At Christmas 1976 the usual Christmas card did not arrive, and they discovered that Mr. King had died in a Brisbane nursing Home on December 12th aged 88. Meanwhile Mr. King's niece had contacted the Rev. James Boyd, Nethybridge, and at the service which followed on April 15th, conducted by Mr. Boyd, those who attended included Mr. McClure, Mr. MacIntyre, Inspector Donald MacKenzie, Kingussie, P.C. Norman Smith, Nethybridge, and Mr. Robert Owen a former Nethybridge bobby.

Dame Aliset, The White Witch

DAME Aliset was a notable white witch in the Abernethy (Strathspey) district. She could predict the weather and the future; she could reveal where hidden treasures were to be found; she gave sage advice to lovers, and could predict the course of a proposed marriage. She was also a competent midwife, medico and vet, and her services were consequently in much demand.

So it was no surprise to her when, as frequently happened, there came a knocking at her door at the dead of night. Lighting a candle she hastened to the door where a little man about four feet high stood holding two ponies. His clothes were old-fashioned and curious, and he told Dame Aliset that his mistress had sent him to beg of her to come and attend to her child who was very ill. Immediately Dame Aliset dressed and packed her basket while questioning the little man closely about his mistress and the child. Then mounting the led pony she followed her escort.

When she came to the secret well of healing she bade the little man stop so that she could fill her flask with the healing water. When he was doing this Dame Aliset, who had already guessed her destination, dismounted and surreptitiously picked a bunch of rowan blossom and slipped it inside her bodice.

In due course they arrived at the Fairy Knoll beside the Spey, and she was ushered inside where she was met by the Fairy Queen. She was led to a bed of furs on which the sick child lay in a high fever. Dame Aliset prepared a mixture from the simples she had brought with the healing waters from the flask, and forced it between the child's lips. Then Dame Aliset ordered that the child should be bathed with the healing water. While the fairies did this Dame Aliset sat and watched. In an hour the child received a second draught of the prepared potion, and again a third draught, after which the child's skin became cool and moist, and she fell into a tranquil sleep. "She will be alright now", said Dame Aliset and prepared to leave after giving the Fairy Queen a few practical instructions.

Immediately Dame Aliset was surrounded by the little people with plenteous offers of gifts of all kinds. Smilingly Aliset refused them all and asked only for their friendship and goodwill. The Fairy Queen only too willingly consented, but in spite of Dame Aliset's protestations insisted that as a token of her gratitude some other gift was necessary, and said that whoever washed in the well of healing and so wished would be restored to their youth again and this, we are told, still applies if you can find the well.

Some say this stream is near the Boiling Well of Rynettin which bubbles up through white sands. There is however a well near Orton in Morayshire which carries a similar legend. From time immemorial the water from this well was famed for its healing powers and was a place of pilgrimage. The pilgrimage was revived in 1978.

Holy Mary of Lurg

IN the beginning of the 13th Century a certain lady of the family of Macintosh of Kylachy was married to Patrick, one of the eighteen sons of Patrick Grant of Tullochgorm, and grandson of the first Laird of Grant. The laird gave Patrick the farm of Lurg on the Braes of Abernethy, above Nethybridge, as a marriage gift. When Patrick of Lurg died he was interred in Duthil Churchyard.

Soon after his wife followed him to the grave. On her deathbed she expressed the wish to be buried in the same tomb as her husband. Her friends protested that the Spey was big in spate and could not be forded. "Go you", she said, "to the waterside to a point opposite Tom Bitlac and a passage will be speedily effected." Her friends complied with her wishes, and when they arrived at the banks of the swollen Spey the waters suddenly divided and the cortege passed over on dry ground. It is said that the solemn occasion was marred by certain members of the company who, on observing a number of salmon leaping about on the dry bed, were tempted to try and capture such an easy haul, but the angry waters resumed their course, and greed almost ended in tragedy. Bigla, the celebrated chatelaine of Tom Bitlac, served the company with bread and wine, and a *te deum* was sung by the whole company for such a miraculous crossing, and for the lives which were nearly lost.

The cortege continued on its way until they reached the top of the ridge above Gartenbeg, and here they rested and a pole about thirty feet long was erected with a fingerboard pointing to where they crossed the Spey. The legend was almost forgotten until in the middle of the last century a crofter called

William Grant, who lived at Slochd about three miles North of Carrbridge, revived it. He was a member of a religious sect called "The Men of Duthil". He was remarkable for his piety rather than eloquence: his religious experiences were deeply subjective. In an environment naturally adapted to the contemplation of the mysterious he cultivated the mystic element in his nature in long and contemplative communion with God. Like a seer from the desert he came forth from his retirement with wonderful visions, but he like all mystics who hover on the border land between the visible and the invisible, was not without his limitations. He was reputed to have the gift of *taibhsearachd* or second sight.

In William's declining years he is said to have had a vision, the reality and significance of which he had not the shadow of a doubt, and on this vision there hangs a tale. In a prophetic dream although he had never seen the spot he described it with uncanny minuteness, even to the size and shape of the bush which marked the spot. He was so strengthened in his belief, and the authenticity of the dream, and the reality of his vision, that before his death he gave instructions that a certain slate slab on Slochd, as revealed to him in his vision, should be hewn out without the aid of hammer or chisel, for the sound of iron or wood instrument must not be heard. It was to be inscribed, and set up as a memorial on the spot of his vision to mark for all generations the miraculous crossing of the Spey.

There were people in Duthil who believed in William's vision and piety, and after his death took steps to give effect to his last request. But forgetting that William had said that hammer and chisel must not be used, they set to with both tools, and completed the work with an inscription. The slab was placed in a cart and accompanied by a solemn procession it was transported on the 9th March 1865 to the spot which is a short distance below the Lagg burn. There the stone bearing the following inscription was duly erected and consecrated by the "Men of Duthil":

ERECTED
AT THE REQUEST
OF

THE LATE
WILLIAM GRANT SLOCK
FOR A MEMORIAL OF A SIGNAL
MANIFESTATION OF THE
DIVINE POWER OF DIVIDING
THIS WATER AND CAUSING
A PASSAGE WHEREBY THE
REMAINS OF A CERTAIN
WOMAN WERE CARRIED
OVER ON DRY GROUND

On the following Sabbath a large crowd gathered to see the stone before attending morning service. From the pulpit the Rev. John Logan, Parish Minister of Duthil, was unsparing in his denunciation of the story as an "abominable lie", and the stone "that puts lies upon God and man". He also denounced in no uncertain manner the Sabbath breakers.

Naturally such a furore attracted attention all over the district, and in certain quarters it was described as a "disgrace to the Parish". It was talked about in every company, and at every fireside. It was discussed, not only in the local papers, but even in *The Scotsman*.

The outcome was the emergence of a vociferous anti-stone party and the Rev. Mr. Logan suffered much spiritual distress. The result was inevitable. Two years after, on the night of 19th February 1867, the stone was broken and the pieces thrown in the river. The identity of the perpetrators of this "act of sacrilege" was preserved, and to this day no one had been able to name the iconoclasts. They have always been referred to as "certain persons". It is on record that a man suspected of being one of the wrecking party was killed in an accident soon after, and this was regarded by many locals as being condign punishment from above.

Within the author's memory he, along with his brother and another companion, used to fish the broken pieces out of the river at low water and place them on the bank. Curiously they always seemed to find their way back into the river. The broken pieces are still to be seen at low water, and miraculously after one hundred and twenty years of river scouring the inscription had not been worn away.

There was supposed to be a curse on anyone who moved the stones, but the author is now almost 80, and his brother in Vancouver almost 82, and both are hale and hearty. The friend, Harry Robertson, died in his late sixties. We seem to have escaped punishment for our interference, but in a recent book on Scottish legends the author claims that within the last twenty years five young boys who had fished out the stones from the river all died soon after. This claim has been carefully investigated but no confirmation has resulted from any local source.

The author also records that during the war a bomber returning from a raid on Germany, and off course had crashed near the spot. The crew included a local man who had fished out the stones in his youth. There is no substantiation locally for this tale either, although it is true that a bomber did crash near the spot.

With regard to the 30 feet pole erected at the spot above Gartenbeg, where the cortege rested, a curious tale is told. One day when two young boys were herding cattle near Gartenbeg one of them, for devilment, pulled down the now rotting pole. That very afternoon he was stricken with a curious malady resulting in serious illness. No one could diagnose the trouble. He was closely questioned about his every activity that day, and when he confessed that he had pulled down the old pole the origin of his malady was at once suspected. He was carried to the spot, and there in his presence the pole was re-erected. Almost at once he rallied, the disease went from him and he returned home in perfect health and spirits.

The legend is reminiscent of the Paray le Monial pilgrimage which occurred about the same time, and a parallel may be seen with Holy Mary of Lurg, a Duthil edition of Marguerite Marie Alacoque. The Church set her seal on Marguerite's devotion, and recommended it to all believers. It might well be said that the "Men of Duthil" did likewise for another Marie. The journey to Garten with the miracle stone was a simple counterpart of the pilgrimage to Paray. Only the ceremonial was different. Here at Garten were no Lords or

Ladies, elegance, no paters, aves or litanies of the Sacred Heart. None of this attended the consecration of the stone on the bank of the Spey as they did the consecration at Paray of the English people to the Sacred Heart. But they were in accord in at least one respect — they were both the result of earnest religious conviction.

The Widow of Strathspey

A LONG time ago on the Braes of Abernethy a woman with second sight was left widowed with a large family to support. In addition to the croft she had a meal mill, and part of the grist was given to the miller in lieu of wages. She regularly visited the mill to make sure that her allocation of the meal was put in the appropriate girnal.

One evening she was delayed at the mill, and it was growing dark as she made her way home. When she came to a little wood the stream running through it was in full spate. The only way across was by tree trunks thrown across the burn, and it was precarious at any time. As she stood in perplexity for a moment she became aware that the figure of her late husband stood on the opposite bank beckoning to her. He waded over, and taking her by the hand led her safely to the other side, and continued to walk beside her through the wood. He rebuked her for being about after dark alone and then disappeared.

When she reached home she recounted her experiences to friends, and showed them the faint mark on her wrist where the hand of her phantom husband had held her.

Everybody was convinced that she had encountered the spirit of her husband who had come to save her from the dangers of crossing the raging water. It was a "speak" in the district for long years after the event.

Tullochgorm

THE Farm of Tullochgorm on the road between Drumullie and Broomhill, and only the breadth of a field from the banks of the Spey, was a place of considerable importance in the 15th and 16th centuries. It had connections with the celebrated Bigla of Tom Bitlac, for it was at Tullochgorm that a second son Patrick MacIain Roy lived, and became the progenitor of the Clan Phadruig Grant of Tullochgorm. When the old mansion was destroyed the household spirit departed. This spirit was no vague apparition but a *gruagach*, or household goddess and family guardian. The word *gruagach* implies a beautiful head of hair, but the Tullochgorm housekeeper also possessed a hairy hand and was consequently known as *Mag Molach* or hairy paw.

The idea of a woman or a female spirit with a hairy paw sounds revolting, but in one who gave such faithful service from one generation to another as *Mag Molach* much could be overlooked. She floated through the air to attend the table, supervised all the daily work, and even saw the master safely home when he was visiting convivial company. On such occasions she considerately simulated the appearance of a small boy carrying a candle to light the way across the moor. If the Laird wished to entertain his cronies in his own home without protestations from his better half Mag Molach grimaced at the goodwife so much that she hastily retired to bed. There may possibly be a relationship between the *Gaelic gruagach* and the Breton *groach*, the name by which the druidic priestesses of Brittany were known. It was their duty to rethatch the temple every year.

The Reel o' Tulloch

A NUMBER of places called Tulloch (from *tulach*, a green knoll) tell for themselves the origin of the Homeric story called the Reel o' Tulloch, but the principal claimant is Tulloch in the foothills south of Nethybridge both on the grounds of tradition and the Gaelic song which was written about the tragedy.

In the 18th century Alan Grant of Tulloch, a petty Chief, had a son Alan, and a strikingly beautiful daughter *Isebail Dhubh Thulaich* (The raven-haired Ishbel of Tulloch).

It is said that when Isebail was born all the guns in the house went off together. When Joan of Arc was born in 1412 the cocks crowed all night long and this was regarded as a good omen. But when Isebail was born the going off of the guns was a bad omen: it presaged blood and death and the midwife who brought her into the world was heard to mutter "*A bhradaig! cuiribh eadar chluasagan i.*" (Wretch! put her between pillows). As she handled the child she continued to mutter "Blood, blood and terror will beset the child if she lives to woman's age".

Isebail survived and grew in beauty and favour. She had admiration and affection of the countryside. She was wooed by many, but she would have none of them, and Alan was ever near to give her his protection. Her parents wished her to marry a Robertson youth who lived nearby, but Isebail had already given her heart to Iain, commonly known as Iain Dubh Gear (short dark Iain), a young man of the proscribed and illstarred MacGregor clan. Their meetings were clandestine, and few and far between, but at each they fell more in love than ever. Alan disapproved of the liaison with a MacGregor, and one day along with seven accomplices he lay in ambush for Iain, but the MacGregor was a strong and able fighter. He beat them off one by one, and took refuge in a barn near Isebail's home. Isebail overheard Alan and his accomplices making plans to beseige the barn, and hastened to warn her lover. When the party arrived, headed by Alan, Iain stood at the door wielding his claymore, while Isebail loaded and reloaded an old musket inside. The murderous mob retreated a little, and when they renewed the assault Isebail handed the musket to Iain crying "Make sure of him in the red coat" and at point blank range Iain fired at the red waistcoat, and mortally wounded Alan who fell dead. Seeing their leader dead the survivors fled the battlefield.

Iain was so elated with his success that he cried, "Love, since I have done this brave deed, haste to give me a draught of beer that I may dance the Tullichan!" But Isebail was in less haste for they remained in the barn for some time in each other's arms. Then Iain composed the song and they were married that night. It was a merry night of song and dance. Tullochgorm, *Seann Triubhais* and the *Cutach-chaol-dubh* made all feet itch, but the Reel o' Tulloch surpassed them all.

More than ever now Iain was a fugative. Hunted from one hiding place to another he was eventually captured while trying to cross the Spey at Blacksboat and summarily put to death.

His head was carried back in triumph to the cell where the dark beauty, Isebail, lay gaoled awaiting the birth of Iain's child. The last sight of Iain's beloved face broke her heart, and she soon followed him to the grave.

She was buried at Kincardine Churchyard and a plain slab, without any inscription marks her grave. The men who were killed in the affray at Tulloch were buried under the knoll called *Tor an Mhortaidh* (Knoll of the Murder).

This is the traditional story. The records of the Court of Justiciary tell rather a different one, but do we want to know?

Ford of the Feinne

LOCH A'an, and the river emerging from it and also the mountain of that name, are frequently but quite erroneously referred to as Loch Avon etc., an anglicized form of the Gaelic *amhuinn* (a river). The origin of the name, however, is much more romantic.

Ath Fhinn was, it is believed, the name of Fionn's wife who was drowned in the river. Before her death the river was called *Uisge Ban* or *Uisge Geal*, meaning clear or pure.

The *Feinne* or *Fianna* was a band of half mythical warriors and hunters greatly admired by mediaeval Gaelic bards and particularly Fionn, their leader. In his poems Ossian Macpherson (more correctly Oisin) refers to Fionn as Fingal. Fionn's death was recorded by Irish historical writers circa 252–283 A.D. One bard wrote lyrically:

> Both poet and chief
> Braver than Kings
> Firm Chief of the Fianna
>
> Foremost always
> Generous just
> of vigorous deeds
> First in song
> a righteous judge
> Firm in rule
>
> Marble his skin
> The rose his cheek
> Blue was his eye
> His hair like gold
> All men's trust
> Of noble mind

On a day when Fionn was hunting without his band his wife accompanied him. When they came to the river called *Uisge Geal*, or *Uisge Ban nan Clachan Sleamhuinn* (White Water of the Slippery Stones) it was a rushing torrent in full spate. Fionn crossed in safety, but when his wife attempted to follow she was swept off her feet and drowned before he could lend any assistance. With sorrow weighing heavily upon him Fionn said

> *Chaidh mo bhean 'sa bhathadh*
> *Air Uisge Ban Nan Clachan Sleamhuinn;*
> *'S bho chaidh mo bhean 'sa bhathadh*
> *Bheirmeid ath-fhinn air an Abhuinn*

(My wife has been drowned in the fair water of the slippery stones; and since my wife has been drowned let us call the River Athfhinn).

A'an was according to legend the name of Fionn's wife but the words might also have had two other translations namely *Ath Fhinn* (Fion's Ford) or *Ath Fianna* (the Ford of the Feinne).

Margaret's Coffin

A SHORT distance below the ridge north-east of the cairn of Cairngorm there is a deep pocket or chest called *Ciste Mearad* (Margaret's chest or coffin) which has an interesting history.

It is said that a lad of the Macintosh clan was condemned to death for a misdeed by the Chief, who in those days had the power of life or death over those of his own clan. The lad's sweetheart begged the Macintosh for mercy, but for all her tears and entreaties he remained adamant, whereupon the girl called a curse upon him and his house, swearing that the estates and chiefship would never more descend from father to son. It is interesting to note that the curse has been fulfilled in this respect.

Losing her reason the girl wandered from home, and tradition has it that her body was found in this remote pocket on the hillside which bears the sombre name of Margaret's Coffin.

Another tradition is that the Margaret who gave her name to the hollow was a Glenmore girl who was in the habit of herding the cattle that grazed up in the high corries in the summer. She passed a good deal of her time searching for Cairngorm stones, and it was in this hollow that she had a *ciste* or chest of treasures. A good find is greatly prized, but the stones are not of great commercial value.

Tradition also relates that if *Ciste Mearad* should ever be bare of snow the Grants of Seafield will no longer own their extensive Estates. It is true that even when all the other corries of Cairngorm are clear a drift of snow still lingers on in *Ciste Mearad*, but is often so discoloured as to be barely recognisable. Even so this probably does in a long hot summer finally disappear too and it is doubtful whether the Grants of Seafield have been unduly worried by its presence or absence.

It is true that in the last twenty years Seafield Estates have shrunk considerably. The pocket drifts over in winter to a great depth. In 1924, when special note was taken, it remained until winter although in August it was only about fifty yards across. In 1914 there was only a very small patch left, weighing perhaps about 8 lbs. The very next day snow fell. However much it shrinks during the summer months the snowfield here has a long life because the first snows in the Cairngorms usually arrive about 10th September.

Barbara Grant of Rhynettan

TULLOCH was noted for its beautiful girls, and another lady of character was Barbara Grant of Rhynettan in whose memory a cairn was erected just past Rhynettan on the road to Glenmore. It is still known as Carn Barbara.

She was of such beauty and sweetness of disposition that she had numerous wooers, one of the most ardent and peristent being a Donald Cameron of Lochaber, a notable fellow, but Barbara spurned his advances as she had given her heart to Seumas Macpherson, a local lad.

But Donald Cameron was a determined, ruthless character, and despite the fact that the wedding day had been arranged he decided to use force where soft words had failed. On the Sunday before the wedding Barbara's family went to the Kirk while she remained at home. Cameron invaded the croft with a tail of followers, and Barbara was abducted along with all the booty that could be removed.

Barbara was a lady of character and they found her none too easy to handle, but when she had been forcibly subdued the party set off post haste for Lochaber. Barbara did not, however, accept defeat easily. Along the trail she surreptitiously tore strands of wool from her shawl and dropped them on the ground to mark the direction, knowing full well that her people would be soon hot in pursuit; but the trail of wool did not satisfy her determination to outwit her abductors, and carefully removing one strongly heeled shoe, and fixing her eye on a point behind the ear of the man who was leading the pony to which she was strapped, she took careful aim and like a flash hit the Cameron with such force behind the ear with the hard heel that tradition says he fell to the ground stone dead. Catching the reins and swinging the pony round Barbara galloped off, and in the ensuing confusion made a good distance before Donald and his henchmen realised what had happened.

Soon Barbara met a strong party of Tulloch men following her wool trail, and after joyful greetings she leisurely made her way home. The Tulloch men continued to pursue the Lochaber abductors who were overtaken in Badenoch. After a fierce fight the Camerons were routed. The Tulloch men returned in triumph with all the stolen booty. Barbara's wedding, we are told, was a joyous occasion.

The Lynstock Gallows Tree

UNTIL about twelve years ago there was an ancient Scots Pine near Lynstock on the Braes of Abernethy which was at one time used as a Gallows Tree. In 1900 it was estimated to be over three hundred years old. The criminals who were hanged from one of its boughs were buried in its shade and the burial mounds are still discernible. Sometimes it was called the Tree of the Brothers because of two brothers who were hanged from it and buried nearby.

The tree eventually became so dangerous that it had to be cut down. A fable circulated for some time that there were superstitious fears in the minds of the local Seafield workers about carrying out the work, but the problem was solved by one of the squad who was not a native of Strathspey. He, it was said, volunteered to cut it down and, it seems, survived any malign influences that may have existed. In fact the felling was done by Donald Carr and an assistant about 1974/75. It was very rotten. Donald Carr, now retired, was Head Forester at Nethy Bridge from 1971 to 1976.

The Old Man of Garten

WITHIN the last one hundred years the natives of the district of Garten and even further afield spoke about *Am Bodach Ghoirtean* (The Old Man or Spectre of Garten) with feelings of dread. Tradition has it that the Bodach was a spirit which dwelt in the woods surrounding Loch Garten and Loch Mallachy, and roamed the countryside in the hours of darkness giving warnings of impending death. He was never seen, but frequently heard. People in the depths of slumber woke up for no accountable reason with feelings of apprehension, and suddenly as they sat up staring into the dreaded darkness they heard the Bodach's peculiar high pitched cry, almost a scream, warning them of the approaching death of a friend or relative.

Donald Macpherson of Tulloch, among others, testified about one hundred years ago the truth of the Bodach's existence by recounting his own experiences. Along with a few close friends he was accustomed to foregather in a certain farmhouse in Tulloch every week to play cards, and have a dram or two. One night, just before midnight, the party ran short of whisky and Macpherson, being the youngest and fleetest member, was ordered to "run the cutter" as it was called; that was to run and fetch further supplies from a nearby *bothan* (bothy) where the "blessings" were illicitly distilled. Having procured the required quantity without difficulty Donald set out for the farmhouse.

It was a cloudless, quiet, starry night, and the path he followed was well-defined. At one point it led through a grassy hollow in which a few low juniper bushes grew. As Donald entered the hollow he became aware of a commotion. It sounded to him like a horse scrambling to its feet. There followed a soft neighing scream as if the horse was terrified. So far Donald was not in the least dismayed. He knew that horses grazed there, and concluding that one had fallen and hurt itself, he stepped towards the juniper. But not a sign of horse or anything else could be seen. Then he thought that some of his friends at the farm had followed him and were playing tricks on him. He called out saying that he knew what they were up to but there was not a syllable of response. Not a sound but the rustling of the leaves. Now he began to shiver with fear as he realised that perhaps he was being confronted by some supernatural agency. He hurriedly left the hollow, and soon entered a clump of birch trees about fifty yards from the farmhouse.

Although Donald was sceptical he nevertheless kept glancing apprehensively over his shoulder. At last when he was just within sight of the farmhouse a louder scream than before seemed to come from the branches above his head. He was startled, but not terrified, and merely quickened his step expecting every moment to see his friends rushing out to ascertain the cause of the scream which, he felt, they were bound to have heard; but when he joined them it was quite apparent that they had not heard anything unusual. He said nothing; perhaps, he thought, it might all have been a figment of his imagination.

About 3 a.m. the party broke up. Donald's home lay in an opposite direction to the others. It was barely half a mile from the farm; five hundred yards along the farm road to the public road, and then some three hundred yards to his home. As he plodded along his mind was occupied by thoughts of his earlier experience. Suddenly, a short distance ahead of him, a huge white object appeared as wide as the road, and faintly luminous. Startled, Donald stopped in his tracks, and looked hard at the strange phenomenon which appeared to his startled gaze like a large billowing white sheet. He was now thoroughly convinced that he was in the presence of the supernatural. The terrifying apparition lay between him and home; to go on was unthinkable. To return to the farmhouse would have been insulting to his manhood. He decided on strategy. Leaving the road he made a wide detour over the heather to the right of the mysterious object. He was relieved to note that the apparition remained in the same spot, but when his attention was distracted for a few moments from keeping the apparition in view by reason of the rough, tussocky heather he heard again to his horror the same blood-curdling scream. Taking to his heels, terror lending speed to his feet, he made for home and never stopped until he fell in a faint on his own kitchen floor.

His mother was awakened by the thud of his fall, and jumping from her bed in alarm hurried to give him attention. When Donald recovered he was roundly scolded for his late hours, and the company he had been keeping. Without a word. he went to bed and it was not until the following day that he recounted his experiences.

The news spread rapidly, and while some held that Donald's encounter had been with the *Bodach choirtean* and news would soon be heard of a death, others scoffed and declared that it was a clear warning against the playing of cards — The Devil's Books as they were called by those who regarded them with disfavour. Be that as it may, it is recorded that the tenant of the farm where the cards were played died very soon after and was buried in Kincardine Churchyard.

At that time the remains and the mourners were conveyed to the Churchyard in wagonettes, and for the funeral in question the conveyances were hired from the *Fear an Taigh Osda* (Innkeeper) at Nethybridge with two spirited white stallions. When the cortege was coming down the road towards Kincardine, and reached the spot where Donald Macpherson had seen the great white apparition, the two stallions began to fight, rearing, biting, kicking, and got so out of control that the hearse overturned, and they lay thrashing on the road. At the same time all heard one of the stallions emitting a loud scream similar to the blood-curdling sounds Donald himself had heard. There is no record of what occurred after this, but the event created a sensation in the district and was discussed at firesides for long afterwards.

The Monster of Loch Garten

IT IS said that Loch Garten is inhabited by a large carnivorous water monster — a cross between a large bull and a stallion with jet black mane, big head, broad back and glaring eyes which used to haunt the burn which flows out of Loch Garten into Loch Mallachy. It was believed that it preyed on young children and lambs. It came out at night, and its roars could be heard echoing amongst the hills.

An old crofter from Nethybridge decided to try and capture the beast. He hitched a rope round an enormous boulder, weighing several tons on the shore of Loch Garten, and bated a gaff with a lamb. He rowed out into the middle of the Loch with the line and heaved the bated hook overboard and went home. All night there was a tremendous thunder and lightening storm above which could be heard the snarls of the infuriated monster. The old man went back in the morning but there was no sign of the huge boulder. All that could be seen was a deep rut leading into the loch where the boulder had been dragged. Since then there has never again been seen any sight or sound of the monster.

The Curse of Altagarroch

THE stream which flows from Loch Mallachy is called the Allt Garbhach (rough stream) and on its way to the Spey it used to turn a meal mill at the Street of Kincardine. It is spanned by a bridge opposite the old mill on the road from Garten to Kincardine and thereby hangs a tale.

Long ago a prospective bridegroom met an untimely end when crossing the stream at this point. His broken-hearted bride forthwith decreed, calling Heaven as witness, that any others bent on matrimony might meet a similar fate if they crossed the stream at the mill.

The curse seems to have been taken seriously because for many years no engaged couple, singly or together, would cross the Allt Garbhach here. Playing safe they would make a long detour to shun the dangers of disregarding the ancient precept.

The Kinveachy Giant and the Bonnet Stone

THE Kinveachy Giant was wicked and evil, and, being wise in his generation, he knew that attempts would be made on his life, so he removed his heart, as giants conveniently can, and concealed it under a stone in the woods of Ben Gulabin in the Forest of Kinveachy. This stone became known as the Bonnet Stone because, as was well known, the only way to kill a giant was for a man to lay his bonnet on that particular stone, and perform a certain ritual which caused the heart to die. Unfortunately the giant's heart kept a careful watch, and on seeing a man wearing a bonnet it hopped out and hid under another stone. He was never killed, and it may well be that the giant still continues to menace the unwary.

There is an ancient tale of Iain Macintosh of Avielochan, a notorious poacher, and Colin Grant who farmed the Croft of Laggantygown. One day Iain shot and gralloched a stag on the low ground below Ben Gulabin. Now he had to get the beast home unobserved, but how. Maybe he thought, *'a lion beag as bheagan mar a dh'ith an cat an t'iasg* (little by little as the cat ate the fish), so he cut the beast in two, and hiding the forequarters in a deep pool in a nearby burn to keep them fresh and free of flies, he shouldered the hindquarters, and cautiously made his way to the west side of Avielochan, and home.

That afternoon Colin Grant went in search of a foal which had strayed, keeping at the same time a sharp eye for Iain, or his life. Near where Iain had gralloched the stag he came on the poor little foal crushed to death by a fallen boulder. These things happen, and Colin wasted no time in false sentiments. He skinned the foal, and went down to the burn to wash his

211

hands, and it was of course, the very pool where Iain had hidden the forequarters of venison. Colin smiled to himself, and replacing the forequarters of venison with the forequarters of foal he went home. Iain returned in the dead of night and retrieved the rest of the carcase. When he discovered how he had been outwitted he was in a black rage, and knowing full well that it must be the work of Colin, and no other, he itched for Colin's blood.

They came face to face a day or two after and a bloody fight commenced, but Colin was overpowered and Iain's *sgian dubh* drained him of his life's blood. Iain buried the body deeply in a peat hag, and set Colin's blue bonnet on a tall standing stone to tell the tale, but no one knows which stone in the Kinveachy Forest is the Bonnet Stone.

There are Bonnet Stones all over the Highlands, but it is of particular interest that a version should have been revived to fit a local tale in a district which is rich in stone circles. The original story concerned an evil giant who hid his soul in a stone, so that he could avoid death at the hands of his mortal foes. There is a heroine in the tale, and making the excuse that she wishes to pay homage to the soul she searches high and low "*C'aite a bheil*"? (Where is it) she asks "*Tha e anns a'Chlach Bhoneid*" (It is in the Bonnet Stone) the evil giant replies. The heroine, traditionally, dresses the stone indicated to her with clothes and ornaments, and professes to pay homage to the spirit within, but only to discover that the giant has moved his soul to another stone, and so her quest goes on until eventually the giant moves his restless soul by mistake into an egg which the heroine crushes, and conquers the wicked giant at long last.

A like tale is contained in the folklore of other countries. The Russian version is very similar in detail to our own.

The Knock of Drumullie Stones

THE Croft called The Knock is within a mile of Boat of Garten. It was the scene of some very mysterious phenomena up to the early years of this century. The house was a good stone and lime building with a slated roof, and chimneys at each end. The tenants were Lachlan Grant and his wife and they had three sons and three daughters who lived with them. They were highly-respected in the district, and Lachie Grant acted as precenter at religious services in the Clachan of Drumullie.

Suddenly stones began to tumble down the kitchen chimney as the family sat round the fire. Sometimes they fell on the hearth, but at other times on the knees of the family. Strangely no injury was ever caused. It was even said that stones followed the male members of the family as they worked in the fields.

The Knock stones became a topic of conversation at every fireside in the district. Some people were sceptical, and brushed it aside as the work of some practical joker. Sometimes the stones came down when there was snow on the ground and certainly there was never the trace of footsteps round the house. Others who were visiting at the time of such an occurrence were quite convinced that a supernatural agency was at work. The family was no doubt upset by these strange inexplicable occurrences, but they were not frightened from their home.

Strangely, however, the whole family died within a few years of each other. The youngest, "Lachie the Knock", was posted missing in the early days of the 1914-1918 Great War. Old Mrs. Grant lived alone for a few years in the house before she too died. The house, now considerably improved, still stands but there has been no repetition of the falling stones since young Lachie went to the War. And it was about that time that a piece of the stone which was erected to Holy Mary of Lurg on the West bank of the Spey below the Knock, and which had been used as a doorstep at the Knock, was returned to the Spey where the other fragments lay. There was a tradition that there was a curse on the broken fragments of the memorial stone.

Gibbon Mór

THE last of the Comyns or Cummins of any account in the Parish of Duthil was Gilbert Comyn, Lord of Glen Chearnach (i.e. the lands watered by the River Dulnan, and over the Deshar ridge to Spey) who by all accounts was a man of prodigious size and strength, and for this reason was called Gibbon Mór. He ruled his lands with a rod of iron.

His chief residence was at Kinchurdy, a farm on the banks of the Spey between Boat of Garten and Aviemore. The house stood on a green which was enclosed by a ditch, traces of which may still be seen. Tradition says that at night a salmon net was cast into a deep pool below the house with a rope attached to it. When a salmon entered the net the rope rang a bell to announce that day's lunch menu. The women in the kitchen were never quite sure, however, if it was a visitor at the front door, or a salmon at the back door.

There was a huge stone at the front door hollowed in the centre like a baptismal font, and it may indeed have been used at one time as such. It was always filled with water for the fowls and thereby hangs a tale.

In those troubled days it was the custom for broken men to seek the protection of the Chief of some other clan, and frequently such men came to Gibbon Mór and begged to be metamorphosed into a Comyn, but before admitting them to his clan a certain ritual had to be observed. Upending them and holding them by the heels Gibbon Mór dipped them three times in the mucky water of the hens' trough, and adjured them in stately tones to thereafter live and do like a Comyn. There was, however, a marked distinction preserved between the Comyns of the blood and those who were baptised in the hens' trough. Henceforth they and their descendents would bear the name *Cuimenech Clach nan Circe* (Comyns of the Hens' Trough).

The trough at Duthil is said to be that very cup-shaped boulder, but although Gibbon Mórs daughter, *Bigla* or *Bitlac* (Matilda) is credited with founding the Church it seems barely credible that such a lump of rock would have been transported, along with all the attendant difficulties, from the Spey to Duthil for no apparent reason.

Tom Bitlac

STRETCHING along the west banks of the Spey at Boat of Garten, from the farm of Dalvoult to the croft called The Knock, there is a range of six glacial moraines. On the lower slopes, and in the hollows between them, circular depressions about ten feet across may be seen. These mark all that remains of the semi-subterranean dwellings of a long-vanished race. The last of the moraines is Tom Bitlac called after the notable Bigla, Bitlac or Matilda, a daughter of Gilbert Comyn, Lord of Glen Chearnach, Kinchurdy and Tom Bitlac. Here at Tom Bitlac in a turf built castle surrounded by a moat she was chatelaine. Little is known about *Bigla* but she appears to have been something of a character. Her simplest acts have taken on legendary proportions as the years have dimmed reality.

Various stones in the vicinity are associated with some tale about her and the founding of Duthil Church. Some of the timbers from Tom Bitlac Castle were, it is said, used in the construction. *Bigla* regularly crossed the hill to worship there and somewhere on the way she had a hiding place for the keys of her castle. Why it was necessary to carry the keys or even hide them it is difficult to say. The very stone became known, and by diligent searching may still be found broken in two lengthways. It is called *Clach an Tuill Bitlac* (Bigla's Stone of the Hole). In all probability the name is purely accidental.

A short distance further on, as you cross from Deshar to Duthil, a large fragment of rock received the name of Bigla's Louping-On-Stone. She is supposed to have mounted her horse from this rock. Here, too, she is said to have received the rents of her estate.

After Gibbon Mór's death about the year 1434 Bigla married her father's hereditary enemy, Sir John Grant of Freuchie and the Glenchearnach race came to an end.

The Clerical Curse of Duthil

ROUND about the year 1700 the Parish minister of Duthil was a godly but undiplomatic man, and as a result did not gain the respect and attention from his flock to which he felt entitled. The Grants of Dalrachney, an important branch of the Clan Grant, had little respect for religion, and none at all for the minister. The antipathy was mutual, and on the occasion of the birth of a son in the Grant family the minister was overheard to remark that yet another demon was added to the tribe. The unwise remark was of course relayed to the Dalrachneys, and the father took such offence that he determined to avenge the insult.

A great banquet and entertainment was laid on for the child's baptism, and a large number of guests were invited. Among the guests was the unsuspecting minister who was dined and wined to such an extent that he had to be carried to bed. When he awoke in the morning sober, but doubtless with a thick head, he was astonished and humiliated to discover that he had been provided with a bedmate for the night, no less a person than his host's dairymaid, who had in all probability been well bribed to play the role of mistress.

News of the incident spread like wildfire, and the poor minister found his position in the community intolerable. He soon took his departure from the Parish of Duthil which he loved so dearly, and tradition has it that when he turned to take a last look at the Parish he prayed on his knees that in order to avenge the injury which had been done to him, and make it a vindication of his innocence, the people of Duthil should be deprived of the services of an ordained minister until the seventh generation. Strange to say it is recorded fact that for seven generations the Parish was noted for strife and discord in the church. This was even so when the author's mother was a young girl in the district about one hundred years ago, although at that time the incumbent was an ordained minister.

Duthil Church

THE Church of Duthill was in early days a prebend of Elgin Cathedral. It has had a long and sometimes stormy history. The present church was built in 1826 in the usual baronial style. The large building in the corner with arched doors and ornamental corners is the imposing mausoleum of the Grants of Seafield. The Chiefs of Grants, later the Earls of Seafield, had a burial ground here since 1585, but the later Earls and their families were laid to rest in the mausoleum.

The first Presbyterian minister was Andrew Henderson, ordained in 1625. Sueton Grant was ejected in 1690. In 1708 Donald Macintosh demitted the charge. It was not filled again until 1719.

Numerous wolf traps used to be found in the district, proving the existence of wolves. A woman who resided at Lochanhully, about a mile west of the church, was returning from a neighbour's with a gridiron in her hand when she met a huge wolf. They stared at each other for a short time before the wolf sprang, but with a well-aimed blow with the gridiron she laid him dead at her feet. Henceforth the place became known as *Clais a' Mhadaidh* (Wolf's Hollow).

Belief in the evil eye is a very ancient superstition and was given much credence in the Highlands. It was held to be an hereditary possession and attributed more to women than men. In the Parish of Duthil as recently as 1902 a local woman is reported to have said: "Plenty of people have the evil eye and hurt both cattle and people with it."

The Cairns of Duthil

THERE are a large number of cairns in the district. The name of the farm of Docharn means the Davoch of the Cairns. Probably the number of small cairns runs into hundreds. Three, however, are enormous; the largest is at *Tom Taigh an Leigh* (the knoll of the doctor's house). The tradition is that every father and mother of an illegitimate child in the parish, was required to bring a stone to the cairn, and thus it rose and continued to rise. One can only conclude from this that in the Parish of Duthil in those days there must have been a flood of births, but few marriages.

The cairn above the farm of Dochlaggie in the Deshar is sixty feet in diameter and about ten feet high. After some careful investigation, about a hundred years ago, no chamber or structure of any kind was found inside. Running north from it, however, for almost forty feet by three feet wide, there is a rough sort of paving. The stones are of different sizes, and no attempt seems to have been made to bed them into the ground. At the north end the paving bends slightly to the east, and at the other end it appears to enter into the cairn itself. It is all very curious, but no theory appears to have been advanced as to their origin or significance.

Near the old house of Inverlaidnan there is a cairn with a similar structure. In this case the cairn is smaller than the one at Dochlaggie, but the paving runs east and west, and goes right through the cairn to emerge at the other side. At the west extremity the paving turns at right angles for a short distance. Surrounding the cairn there is a circle of stones similar to the paving. In the centre of the cairn there is a well formed short cist with a large stone covering it. When first excavated the cist contained human remains. There is support for the idea that there is an anatomy of the cairns; that is, that they are not just heaps of stones but are constructed on a different plan. The Caithness cairns are of an entirely different character, but it is quite probable that the cairns of different districts may possess distinctive characters. The work on constructing such cairns must have been massive, and it is frustrating that we cannot decipher their meaning.

The Ghost of Castle Grant

CASTLE Grant was for a number of years a ruin but it is now being restored. In its heyday it was a very fine pile. One small, insignificant bedroom in the old tower was reputedly haunted. It was reached by a stone staircase, richly carpeted with ancient Grant tartan. The bedroom was hung with rich tapestry said to have been woven by twenty-two ladies who once lived in exile at Castle Grant.

A gentle little lady was said to appear through the tapestry occasionally. She went through the motions of washing her hands, and then darted through a door on the other side of the room.

No one has ever been sure of the lady's identity, although it was popularly believed that she was the ghost of Barbara Grant, a daughter of a Sixteenth Century Chief of Grant. A door in the room opened into a dark closet, and it was said that Barbara was held prisoner in the dark closet by her father because she refused to marry the man her father had chosen for her. Here in this dark cell she died rather than yield to a man she could not love.

Little John MacAndrew

LITTLE John MacAndrew, or as he was called in Gaelic *Iain Beag MacAindrea*, was very small in stature but had tremendous courage and resource, and his skill with the bow and arrow was known all over the Highlands.

While on a foray to Strathdearn the Laird of Achluachran, with a strong body of men, was on his way west with cattle he had lifted from the lands of Rose of Kilravock. At Cro-Clach in Strathdearn, they were overtaken by Rose of Kilravock and Macintosh of Kylachy with a numerous following of clansmen. *Iain Beag* who was also in Strathdearn at the time was prevailed upon by Kylachy to support him with his celebrated skills. Iain agreed, and gave a fine account of himself in the fierce fight that followed. The Chief himself fell, mortally wounded by an arrow from Iain's bow. When Kylachy saw this he shouted unwisely in a loud voice, "*Tapadh leat fhein Iain Beag MacAindrea bho Dalnahaitnich, 'se do laimh rinn sud* (thanks to yourself little John MacAndrew from Dalnahaitnich, it was your hand that did it). *Iain Beag* was instantly aware of Kylachy's motives, and angrily retorted, "*Mile malachd ort air do theanga Iain Coillsach's eagal ort*" (a thousand curses on your tongue Iain Kylachy and you afraid).

Kylachy's ruse was to draw particular attention to the part Iain had played, knowing that the people of Lochaber would seek revenge on Iain, and perhaps leave Strathdearn free of further molestations. Not a man in the raiding party was left alive, except for a young boy who acted as a scout, and who watched the affray from a distance. He promptly set off for home to tell the tragic tale.

When Iain Beag returned home to his croft at Dalnahaitnich,

which still stands on the Dulnain a few miles west of Carrbridge, he improvised a hiding place in a great, old, heavily branched fir tree that stood near the door of his house, and in it he placed his bow and arrows in readiness for what he knew would inevitably come. Sure enough, not long afterwards, he spied a group of strangers in a wood a little distance from the house, and he knew at once their purpose. They approached and spoke civilly to him little guessing that the insignificant little fellow they addressed was their quarry. They asked for directions to the house of *Iain Beag* MacAindrea, and he smartly led them to the farmhouse. When they entered Iain's wife knew instinctively who they were. She treated them hospitably with food and drink, and then enquired their errand. They told her that they had come to see her husband on a business matter, whereupon she cuffed Iain on the ear, and told him to go and fetch his master who, she told the visitors, was herding up the hill. Out went Iain and climbed up to his refuge in the tree, and got his bow and arrow ready. After a suitable time had passed his wife peered out of the window, and told the visitors that her man was outby. Quickly they arose, and eager to avenge their chief without delay rushed from the house, but one by one they were slain until only one man remained. To him Iain said "*Rachaibh dhachaidh 's innis do naigheachd*" (go home and tell your tale). There is no record of any further attempts on Iain's life, but a monument to the gallant archer still stands at Dalnahaitnich, and the mounds of the slain are still discernible by the side of the Dulnain.

Another version refers to him as *Ruairidh Troich* (Roderick the Dwarf). He did not belong to the district, but was brought to it by an eagle which had snatched him as an infant from his parents who were working in the field. His poor parents never expected to see him again. He was found near Dalnahaitnich by the tenants of that time, and brought up as one of their own. Roderick grew so slowly that he never exceeded Tom Thumb size, but what he lacked in stature he made up for in skills. He became a prosperous farmer, held large stocks of cattle, and married a local girl. He was such a skilful archer that it was said he could stick an arrow into the one that preceded it.

The Water Kelpie's Bridle and the Mermaid's Stone

THE story was told to Sir Thomas Dick Lauder, author of *The Moray Floods: Tales of the Highlands and Highland Legends,* and two friends round about the year 1880 by Grigor Willox MacGrigor, better known as Willox the Wizard, who lived at Gaulrig in Glen Avon, some two miles or so from Delavorar. When each of the visitors to his rude cottage was introduced in turn Sir Thomas was struck by what appeared to be a transient gleam of electricity shooting from the old man's eyes into each of their faces individually. It felt, he said, as if the look had penetrated into the inmost recesses of their souls; as if by long practice in the study of mankind the Wizard was able to read their characters and thoughts like a book. He bowed with grave courtesy to each of them in turn.

After the usual preliminary salutations Sir Thomas expressed a desire to see the famous magic Kelpie's bridle and mermaid's stone. After eyeing Sir Thomas with a searching look the old man said "You shall see them both sir; to such a gentleman as you I cannot refuse a sight of them though are hardly to be seen by vulgar eyes, and never to be handled by vulgar hands."

With that he went into the cottage and returned with his bridle and stone saying, "Here are the wonderful implements of my art".

Sir Thomas requested the Wizard's permission to make a quick sketch, and hoped that by doing so it would not affect their virtues, but the Wizard assured him that their virtues could not be tarnished by human hands. The stone was a circular flatish lense, about three inches in diameter and of semi-opaque crystal. It resembled a bullseye which was at one time used for transmitting light through the deck of a ship into the smaller apartments below.

The bridle was a flat piece of brass, annular in the middle with two lobe-like branches spinning from it in two curves outwards, the wider part of the lobe being slightly recurved inwards, so that when held flat it presented the appearance of two leaves. Attached to the ring part, but loose on it, were two long doubled pieces of flat brass, and between them a short leather thong by a fastening so intricate it might have rivalled the Gordian Knot. It was not apparent to the visitors what practical purpose it served. It bore not the slightest resemblance to any bridle they had ever seen.

But the Wizard soon enlightened them. He told them that his grand-uncle MacGregor who lived on the banks of the Dulnain river near Dulnain Bridge was so devoted to the study of the metaphysical that he became famed far and wide for his power over the world of spirits. His name was never mentioned without reverential awe. He walked much alone in the wilds surrounding his home, and it was believed that during these solitary walks he held converse with spirits of the other world.

One evening as he walked along the shores of Loch an Dorb the sky was calm but the air was hot and sulphurous. The sun sank in a blood red haze which MacGregor with his keen senses knew to be portentous. Wrapped in plaid, he rested against a large boulder and gazed expectantly at the sinking sun, fortifying himself the while for an adventure in which he knew instinctively that he would be involved. Suddenly there was a tremendous turbulence in the black waters of the loch, and huge waves dashed on the shore without any apparent cause. He remained resolute, gazing fixedly at the centre of the vortex, when, more to his delight than astonishment, an enormous beautifully proportioned black horse approached him through the waves. On reaching the shore he pranced along the strand snorting, pawing the ground, and neighing with thunderous tones. Blue lights stabbed from his nostrils and his eyes gleamed like stars. MacGregor knew that here without the shadow of a doubt was the *Each Uisge*, the Water

Horse or Kelpie himself. His heart beat high with a rare hope. He moved to a position behind the boulder, and used certain charms to aid in his concealment. As the *Each Uisge* curvetted grandly past him MacGregor sprang out, and seizing the bridle with one hand he raised his sgian dubh with the other hand and cut it from the Kelpie's head. Instantly the Kelpie was metamorphosed into a man of formidable proportions and forbidding appearance and in a voice like thunder he roared, "Give me back my bridle thou son of earth". "No", cried MacGregor, "I have won it, and I shall keep it". "Then" roared the enraged spirit, "you and it shall never enter your house together".

Whereupon MacGregor took to his heels and raced for home with all the speed he could command, the raging spirit close on his heels, the hot fetid breath almost suffocating him. He was fortunate that the fiend had lost in speed by his metamorphosis else MacGregor would have had little chance of keeping ahead. It seemed indeed that he had acquired some measure of speed from the magical virtue inherent in the bridle, for he seemed, to his own surprise, to flow rather than run over the bogs, knolls and heather that lay between him and his home, but even so his supernatural speed did little more than keep him a few paces ahead of the fiend roaring at his heels. When they at last reached the house MacGregor was too wise in his knowledge of the supernatural to enter by the wide open door. Luckily his wife was close by an open window, and shouting to her "Hello, catch this in your apron", he adroitly threw the bridle into her lap, and so cunningly avoided the prediction which the kelpie had earlier uttered.

No sooner did the fiend perceive that he was outwitted than he uttered a shreik which was heard far and wide in Strathspey, and disappeared from sight. To this day the *Each Uisge* has never again been seen by mortal man, but the bridle was handed down to Willox.

The story of how the mermaid's stone was acquired is no less extraordinary than that of the bridle. The stone came to the wizard from his natural grandfather who gained it by the superhuman powers that he too possessed. After frequent visits to the sea his grandfather at last discovered the spot where a beautiful mermaid was wont to emerge to sport in the shadows, and sit on a rock combing her long tresses, singing the while exquisite melodies quite unconscious of the observer close at hand. At last after arming himself with certain magical spells the grandfather emerged from his hiding place in the rocks and stealthily approached the rock upon which she sat, and clasped her eagerly in his arms. Despite her struggles and cries of alarm he carried her ashore where she became quiet and meek and utterly helpless.

Delighted with his prize he brought her home in triumph. He made a soft bed for her in the rafters, but unwillingly took the precaution of tying her to the couples. Apart from this restraint he lavished so much attention on her that his wife became jealous, and more perhaps out of spite than wickedness she began to encourage the attention of a young man with whom she had previously had an affair. Her husband, despite his powers, was completely blind to the fact that his wife had taken a lover who visited the cottage while he was absent. But one day he returned so unexpectedly that the young man had to dive under the bed. For a moment the lady was in a state of consternation, but she was astute and her wits were sharp as a result of living with such a husband. "I dreamed a strange dream last night", she said smiling gaily. "I dreamed that I put my hands over your eyes and yet you saw as well as if they had not been there".

"Come, try them my dear", replied her husband to humour her. "I believe I can see as far into a millstone as most people".

"No doubt you can" said his wife gleefully clapping her hands firmly over his eyes. "Now can you see?"

"No", replied her husband, "not one whit".

"Stay a little", she cried, laughing joyfully. "Depend upon it this miraculous light will come to you at last".

"Aye, Aye", cried he, and struggling free he kissed her heartily. "I see well enough now".

But the poor man's vision came too late, for the lover

231

seizing the opportunity so cunningly afforded him made his escape undetected. Up in the rafters the mermaid shrieked with unearthly laughter and to divert her husband's attention the lady again with creditable presence of mind threw down the flat stone which in those days was used as a girdle and broke it into pieces. Her loud lamentations quickly diverted her husband's attention from the mermaid's mysterious merriment.

The poor mermaid pined, and sighed so much for her native element that at last her captor was moved to pity. "Take me down to the sea, and put me into the waves just three yards from the shore and it shall be far better for thee than all the good thou can'st gain by keeping me here".

Taking her down from the rafters the wizard's grandfather carried her to the sea and wading three yards in from the shore put her gently down in the water. The mermaid's joy in finding herself back in her native element, after being hung up and smoked like a haddock for so long, knew no bounds, and to show her gratitude for his compassion she gave him wise counsel in these words. "Travel not so oft, or so far from home again. Ill luck tends that home whence the master often wanders. Dost thou remember my loud laugh on that day when thy wife broke the girdle stone? It was because she made a fool of thee by blinding thine eyes that her lover might escape unseen. Be wise in future, never leave home; and when you go back now look among the straw where the broken bits of the girdle stone were thrown, and you will find that which will be a treasure to you and your children for ever".

With that she dived into the sea, and he saw her no more. The wizard's grandfather returned home crestfallen, but on searching in the straw as the mermaid had directed him he found the very stone which has for generations been the agent in performing so many wonders. There is no mention of the grandfather confronting his wife with her infidelity!

When the name of MacGregor was proscribed some of the clan adopted the name Willox. John Willox is recorded as being tenant of Easter Raigmore farm between 1718 and 1735. His grandson became Factor of the Seafield Estates in

Strathspey, and his great grandson, who resumed the name
MacGregor was a distinguished doctor in London. He was
appointed physician to George IV and knighted for his
services. His illegitimate grandson, Willox the Wizard,
preferred to follow the unusual career of horse doctor and
wizard. He worked in his cures with plain water, a magic
pebble and other small artefacts. His death in 1833 was
recorded in the *Inverness Courier*.

The Cairn of Remembrance

ON the lands of Monaltrie, on the north side of the Dee, in a narrow pass where there is not more than sixty yards from the River to the foot of a high steep rocky hill stands *Carn na Cuimhne* (The Cairn of Remembrance). The military route is carried along the foot of the hill and through the pass. Tradition is that in times of danger the Chiefs raised their men, and marching through the pass made every man lay down a stone at this point. When they returned the stones were recounted by which means it was known how many were in the affray, and how many returned. "*Carn na Cuimhne*" has been since then the watchword of the country.

Then every man capable of bearing arms was obliged to have his arms, a bag of bannocks, and a pair of new mended shoes always in readiness. At the moment danger was apprehended a flake of wood called a *croistarich* or *criostarra* (a signal of defiance before commencing battle), one end dipped in the blood of an animal, the other end burned as an emblem of fire and sword was put in the hands of the person nearest to the point where the alarm was given. He ran with all speed, and handed it to his nearest neighbour male or female, who continued on a route previously arranged, and so from hand to hand until the whole country was roused, upon which every man picked up his arms and knapsack, and reported at *Carn na Cuimhne*. If a row or squabble arose at a market the slogan "*Carn na Cuimhne*" had such influence over the minds of the people that the very mention of it would bring the natives to the assistance of the person assailed.

The Ghost of Sergeant Davies

IN 1754 Duncan Terig (probably from the Gaelic *dearg*, meaning red) alias Clark, and Alexander Ban MacDonald were charged with the murder of Sergeant Davies, an English Redcoat in Braemar.

The sworn testimony of Alexander Macpherson of Inverey is curious and may be found in the official account of the trial which was held at New Sessions House, Edinburgh. In it Macpherson swore that the ghost of Sergeant Davies appeared to him and indicated to him where his mortal body lay.

After the '45 Rebellion the district of Mar, like many other areas of the Highlands, was in a state of unrest, and a detachment of eight foot soldiers under Sergeant Davies was sent from Aberdeen to Braemar. Another party under a Corporal was stationed at the Spittal of Glenshee. Their duty was to take possession of any arms and tartan that might be used and worn. Both parties met weekly at a previously arranged spot in the Cairnwell Pass.

Sergeant Davies was an enthusiastic sportsman, and had the habit, despite warnings, of the dangers involved in leaving his men and going hunting or fishing by himself. Something of a dandy, Sergeant Davies wore silver buckles on his shoes, silver knee buckles, silver buttons on his specially woven doublebreasted vest, a silver watch and gold rings on his fingers. Imprudently he carried on his person a green silk purse encased in leather containing fifteen gold guineas and some silver.

On September 28th 1749, he set out early with four men to meet the Glenshee patrol. In the afternoon four men returned alone to their quarters, and reported to the Sergeant's wife that they had seen her husband on the hill and heard a shot. When he did not return that night a party set out, and made an exhaustive search of the ground where the Sergeant had last been seen. For days the party scoured the hills but found not a single clue. In June 1790 Alexander Macpherson of Inverey began to be troubled by the apparition of a man clad in blue. Rising from his bed he followed the apparition to the door where the apparition told him that he was the ghost of Sergeant Davies who had been brutally murdered. He told Macpherson exactly where his mortal body lay, and begged him to give him a decent burial. He added that Donald Farquharson, a good friend, would help him. The body was found in a peat hag in the hill precisely as the apparition had explained. It was fully clothed, but the silver adornments had been cut off.

Macpherson reported his discovery to two local men, John Shaw of Daldownie, and John Gruer of Inverey. Now the very morning of the day he disappeared this same John Gruer had been warned by Sergeant Davies that he must no longer wear his tartan coat. Here was a pretty kettle of fish and the two were disturbed by Macpherson's news. They advised him to go stealthily and bury the body, and say nothing as it could not be carried to a Kirk unheard, and the noise might hurt the country which was already under suspicion of being a rebel country. But Macpherson took no action until the apparition appeared again begging, and insisting that he must bury the body. When Macpherson asked the apparition who had committed the murder the ghost named Clark and MacDonald. He then sought out Donald Farquharson, and together they buried the body on the hill where it was later exhumed by the Authorities.

The two men were duly apprehended, and brought to trial. During his cross-examination Macpherson was asked in what language the ghost had spoken to him. He replied that it was in the Irish language (meaning Gaelic). The messages may have been received telepathically by Macpherson who might well have been psychic. He went on to say that having given the names of the murderers the ghost immediately vanished.

Macpherson was at the time sleeping in his employer's house, and Isobel MacHardy, his employer's wife, testified later in Court that she had also seen the ghost that night, and it frightened her so much that she pulled the bedclothes over her head. Next morning Macpherson assured her that it would not trouble her again.

The accused were found not guilty and acquitted. It seems unusual justice for that time.

The Black Colonel

NEAR the Clachan of Inverey, six miles West of Braemar, a heap of rubble is all that remains of the stronghold of the Farquharson's of Inverey. They were a notable family in the Highlands of Aberdeenshire, said to be descended from Farquhar, a son of John Shaw of Rothiemurchus, circa 1370. A celebrated ancestor was *Fionnlagh Mór* (Big Finla or Finlay), a man of prodigious strength who was killed at the Battle of Pinkie (1547) when carrying the Royal Standard of Scotland. Many were the tales that used to be recounted in Mar about Big Finla.

Probably the most outstanding descendant was John the third Chief who was a tall, swarthy man which earned him the nick-name *An Coirneal Dubh* (The Black Colonel). He was a man of outstanding courage in battle. His time was spent mainly at Iverey Castle, where he lived with a small bodyguard under the leadership of Alasdair MacDougal. When Alasdair was required to attend on his master the Black Colonel did not shout, or whistle, or ring a bell; he summoned with a pistol shot at a target on the wall.

In the troubled days of his time the Black Colonel was surrounded by enemies. One of his remarkable feats was to ride his black mare from the Pass of Ballater up the steep rocky hill on the north side of the Pass in order to escape from two companies of Government dragoons converging on him from each end of the Pass. Looking at the steep boulder-strewn slope it is difficult to believe that such a feat was performed. It is, however, an indisputable fact that his escape from his pursuers did occur in this way.

On another occasion he eluded his pursuers by a hairsbreadth. Rushing stark-naked from his hideout to the River Ey which was in full flood he cleared the river in one mighty leap. The old, hump-backed bridge which carried the old road across the Ey, near the spot where he made his historical leap became known as *Drochaid Leum* (Bridge of the Leap). The spot is about one mile upstream of the present bridge over the river.

Much of the time at Inverey was occupied in preparing for war, and when Viscount Dundee requested the Colonel to raise an Army no second bidding was needed. Alasdair MacDougal was instantly dispatched to every corner of the Farquharson's lands, bearing in his hand the fiery cross, that is two pieces of wood in the form of a cross, one end burning the other dipped in blood, and as he ran he shouted, "*Carn na cuimhne, Carn na cuimhne*" (cairn of remembrance), the Farquharson's battle cry. In a short time the clan had mustered at Inverey Castle, and marched off to war headed by the Chief himself.

At the Battle of Killiecrankie in 1689 many Farquharsons were killed, but the Colonel and his bodyguard escaped, and went into hiding at Inverey where they remained unmolested for a short time. One night, when they had all retired, there was a loud knocking at the courtyard gate, and when Alasdair MacDougal cautiously investigated he discovered an old woman who had come from Braemar to warn the Colonel that the Redcoats were on his trail. Leaping from his bed, and gathering together all that he might urgently require, he, along with the faithful Alasdair set off up Glen Ey, leaving the rest of the bodyguard to fight a rearguard action and delay the Redcoats. They were soon overpowered and the Castle set on fire, and in the light from the burning building a heavily cloaked figure was seen to dash from the building. Thinking that they had the Colonel in their grasp at last the soldiers gave chase, only to find that their captive was *Annie Ban* (fair Annie), the Colonel's housekeeper, who, by her courageous ruse gave her Chief more time to make his escape. After questioning her, and finding her of little help, she was allowed to go free.

On the top of *Creag A'Chait* (The Cat's Rock), the hill above the Castle, the Black Colonel and Alasdair watched the burning Castle, Alasdair with sorrow, but the Colonel with glee. He burst into laughter, and told Alasdair that he had put all the gunpowder in the Charter room, and locked it against such an eventuality. He had hardly finished speaking when there was an explosion which was heard over a long distance.

How many of the Redcoats were killed by the Colonel's ruse was never known, but a small band was observed moving about the ruins. They remained at Inverey for a short time, and hunted daily in all directions for the fugitives, who all the time were hiding in a cave out of the rocks beside the River Ey, known to this day as the "Colonel's Bed". Secretly, *Annie Ban* managed to bring them food, and they were never discovered.

When the Redcoats left the Black Colonel came out of hiding to inspect the ruins of his home, and vowing vengeance rallied a band of his clansmen, and in a skirmish below Creag Choinnich at Braemar put the Royalist soldiers to flight.

He died about the year 1698. He had clearly expressed a wish that he would be buried with his ancestors in the little graveyard at Inverey, but for some unknown reason he was buried at Castleton of Braemar in the massive Farquharson vault with all the honours due to a Chief. But the Black Colonel's wishes were not to be denied even in death. The day after his funeral the coffin was discovered with horror lying beside the open grave. Three times it was buried, and three times it came to the surface. Only then was the Colonel's wishes recalled, and it was decided to bury him at Inverey. The road to Inverey was blocked at the time but a raft was made for a bier, and the Colonel's remains went to their resting place by the River Dee.

The old churchyard is now overgrown and ruinous, and no stones are to be found marking the graves of the Farquharsons of Inverey, or their retainers including Alasdair MacDougal and *Annie Ban*. The Colonel's broadsword and targe are preserved at the seat of the present Chief, Colonel Aylmer Farquharson of Invercauld House.

The years passed, and one day when men were digging a grave in the Churchyard they accidentally broke into the crumbling coffin. Being less trustworthy than they might have been they pocketed the Colonel's teeth, perhaps hoping to sell them as souvenirs or talismans, but that night the ghost of the outraged Colonel appeared to them both and demanded the return of his teeth. Early next morning this was done.

A branch of the Mackenzies of Kintail lived at Dalmore, near where Mar Lodge now stands. The first Mackenzie of Dalmore married a daughter of Finla Mór of Inverey and the lands remained in possession of the Mackenzies for one hundred and forty years.

One of the last of the race was *Seumas na Pluic* (James of the Blub or Fat Cheek). He was a bitter enemy of the Lochaber cattle thieves who periodically raided Mar. On one occasion, when they had lifted a *creach* in Glen Ey, Seumas and his two sons set off in pursuit. When they had almost overtaken the band Seumas told his two sons to stay where they were and he would go forward to parley with the *Cearnach Dubh* (Black Freebooter) the renowned chief of the caterans. They were to watch him closely and if he raised his hand to his brow they were to fire without warning at the enemy. In the course of trying to persuade the cateran chief to give up the stolen cattle for a certain sum of money Seumas unguardedly lifted his hand to his bonnet. His sons, thinking this was the prearranged signal opened fire and killed the cateran who was on guard at the bothy door while his companions rested inside. Whereupon the *Cearnach Dubh*, believing that this was an act of treachery, seized the guard's gun and killed *Seumas na Pluic* where he stood. In the fight which followed *Seumas'* two sons were killed also.

The bothy has for long been just a heap of stones but the cairn which was erected on the spot where *Seumas* fell can still be seen in the Alltan Odhar.

The Gallows Tree was a fine old Caledonian Pine which stood on the left hand side of the road from Braemar to Inverey about two hundred yards west of the Mar Lodge entrance. Unfortunately a gravel pit was opened beside the tree, and in the course of time, its roots undermined, it fell into the pit and died. It was, however, pulled upright by interested parties, gaunt and lifeless, and held with wire stays.

It is believed that before the Farquharsons became overlords at Inverey the lands were in the possession of an old family of Lamonts, who had come from Argyll. They became fewer in number as their lands were taken over.

In the 15th century on this very Gallows Tree a Lamont of Inverey, who lived with his widowed mother, was hanged for a misdemeanour, or perhaps no misdemeanour whatever, by the Farquharsons who, by this time, were all powerful in the district. His mother pleaded for his life but when she saw that her entreaties were unavailing she cursed the Farquharsons in Gaelic and predicted their doom:

> This tree will flourish high and
> Green as it grows today,
> When from the banks o' bonny Dee
> Clan Fionnlagh's all away.

The prediction was fulfilled almost to the letter. One by one the Farquharson families disappeared from the district — Farquharson of Inverey, of Monaltry, of Auchendryne, Alanquoich, Tullochcoy, and finally Invercauld became extinct in the male line.

The Tree of the Gold

ON the slopes of Carn Crom to the north of Luibeg in the Forest of Mar stands *Craobh an Oir* (Tree of the Gold), an old gnarled fir of great age where tradition says a treasure of gold was once buried. It was hidden there by a Laird of Dalmore in Mar after raiding Lochaber. He first buried it in the Garbh Choire Dhé of Braeriach, and later moved it to the old fir in Glen Lui Beg where he could keep it under close surveillance. In the course of time the sale of certain land in Cromar interested him, and lifting the treasure again he set out on his journey of inspection. When he reached the top of Culbleen he could see that Cromar was little better than bog and rock. "*Na leigheadh Dia gun cuireadh mise m'or 'san uisge*" (God forbid that I should throw my gold into the water) exclaimed Dalmore, and turned for home with his treasure. This time he hid it on Carn Geldie and placed over it a huge stone on which was carved a horseshoe, and there, it is said, it still remains.

King Malcolm and the Herd Boy

DURING the reign of Malcolm Canmore, the Constable of Kindrochit Castle kept a wild boar called *Tad Losgann* for the King's amusement. He had captured it when hunting in Glen Quoich, and had constructed for it on the banks of the River Clunie a den which was part natural, and part artificial. Tad Losgann was one of the sights of Kindrochit, and the King always paid a visit to the den.

The Constable was a hard man who held the power of life and death over the people. He had little sympathy for the poor, and he decreed that every family in the district must in turn supply a live cow to appease the boar's hunger which meant great hardship for most people, most of whom were very poor.

When it came to the turn of Mrs MacLeod, a poor widow who lived in Glen Slugan with her son Sandy, a youth of about fifteen, she was almost demented because the cow was her most treasured possession next to Sandy, and it had taken a long time to save enough money to buy it. It had been a hard struggle to make ends meet since her husband, a noted bowman, had been killed in a fight at Corriemulzie when Sandy was only a few months old. When Sandy overheard her crying in indignation and distress that if Donald had still been alive he would have put an arrow through the fat brute's heart, he determined to do something about it.

Sandy had inherited his father's gifts with the bow, and had made a name for himself in the district. He was constantly practising while herding in the hills. Quietly he set about his task and first made three new arrows well barbed and skilfully feathered. Then he went up Carn Liath and shot a capercailzie which he carefully hid. That night he could not sleep, and an hour before dawn he crept out of the house, collected his bow and arrows, and set off for *Tad Losgann*'s den. The guard was on the castle wall, but being a skilful stalker, Sandy crept forward soundlessly on his hands and knees until he was on the edge of the den. There was no sign of the boar. He must be asleep in the dark sheltered corner of the pit. Carefully, and without a sound, Sandy swung the bird and threw it across the den to the dark corner. It seemed like ages before the boar emerged, sniffed the air and then observing the carcase immediately started to devour it. Now was Sandy's chance. Carefully taking aim he fired and shot Tad Losgann through the heart. With a wildly beating heart Sandy sped home.

Next day there was uproar at Castleton of Braemar when it was discovered that the Constable's boar had been shot dead with an arrow through his heart, and the duty guard was straight away put in chains for his apparent negligence.

There was consternation in the Castle for the King was coming the following day, and who knew what the mysterious bowman's next deed might be, perhaps the guard, perhaps the Constable, perhaps even the King himself. The bowman must be found without loss of time. Secretly the people rejoiced, and hoped that their deliverer would not be discovered. But the Constable was a determined man, and after closely examining the arrow that had killed *Tad Logann*, and noting the peculiar feathers, he gave orders that every cottage in the district was to be searched until an arrow with the same feathering was discovered.

Such a search had not occurred to Sandy, and before becoming aware of what was afoot the searchers discovered similar arrows in the house and he was taken to the Castle, put in chains and cast into the dungeon.

Next day he was brought before the Constable who was greatly surprised at his youth, but condemned him nevertheless to be hanged the following morning on the gallows on Creag Choinnich.

The poor old widow was overcome with grief, but she was equally determined. She knew that any appeal for mercy to the Constable would be in vain so her appeal must be to the King. Knowing that the King was expected the next day she trudged up the Cairnwell Pass so that she would be sure to encounter him on his way to Castleton. Perished to the bone she endured that night and all the next morning, but in the later afternoon she was heartened to see the King's cavalcade approaching. When the party reached her she flung herself at the King's feet, and pleaded for her son's life. Touched by her anguish and sincerity the King promised to look into the matter, and commanded her to follow him to Kindrochit where, as he arrived, poor Sandy was being led out to his execution. The King at once stopped the execution party, and after words with the Constable, Sandy and his mother were summoned before them to be told of the King's decision on the matter. Sandy would be given the chance to save his life if he could shoot a peat balanced on his mother's head.

It was an appalling situation for the boy, but he had a strong nerve and a stout heart, and he knew that he must not fail. Trembling, the poor widow was made to stand on the rocky ledge across the Clunie, from which Sandy had shot *Tad Losgann*, with a peat balanced on her head, while Sandy stood on the drawbridge. He asked for his own bow, and the two arrows which had been confiscated when all the houses had been raided. Taking a deep breath, and stealing himself for the ordeal, he raised his bow and took aim. Across the water his mother was able to muster an encouraging smile at her son. The arrow sped swiftly on its way; the peat was knocked from his mother's head, and she emerged from the ordeal unscathed.

The King summoned Sandy and said, "A splendid shot but why two arrows? If you had missed with one you know that you would have been hanged." With greater courage than discretion Sandy replied, "Sire, if I had killed my mother with the first arrow, the second arrow would have killed you". There was a gasp of dismay from the assembled company, but the King's admiration for the boy's skill, courage and honesty was such that he laughed heartily. "Well said, well said," he cried, "You are a hardy one, so henceforth Hardy you will be by name and when you are older you will join my archers."

So Sandy returned with his mother to the croft in Glen Slugan, but he did not become one of the King's archers for never again did he ever draw a bow.

Hardy he was called to the end of his life, the progenitor of all the Hardy's that have followed since.

Kindrochit Castle

BEHIND the shop, near the bridge over the River Clunie at Braemar, are foundations and ruins of the eleventh century castle of Kindrochit. Here, according to legend, a ghostly company sits round a table piled with skulls and inestimable treasure.

King Malcolm III of Scotland, nick-named *Ceann Mor* (Big Head), 1058-1093, who was killed at the siege of Alnwick, built Kindrochit Castle as a hunting lodge and bestowed on his Captain of the district the Earldom of Mar.

It was once a hunting seat of Robert I of Scotland. It was strategically placed to guard the Cairnwell and Stormont passes, and connect the south with the turbulent north. Its importance increased with the years, and in 1390 part of the old building was pulled down and a massive stone tower built by Sir Malcolm Drummond, the Constable of the castle. He also built a massive bridge across the River Clunie. For over a quarter of a century the Royal Standard flew over the battlements. It was strong and flourished in 1400, but by the beginning of the sixteenth century it was becoming derelict, and by 1680 a complete ruin. Tradition says that the *An Galar Mór* (the great disease or plague) broke out in the castle, and terrified that the pestilence might spread the people barred the castle gates, and refused the garrison permission to come out. It is said that cannons were brought over the Cairnwell from Atholl. The castle was reduced, and the garrison massacred. As late as the sixteenth century anyone suspected of carrying the plague was hanged on the nearest gallows. It is possible that there may be some truth in the tradition.

Years passed then, in 1746, a Hanoverian soldier was

lowered into the vaults to search for reported treasure. Frantic signals brought him to the surface white and trembling. He reported that he saw a huge congregation of ghostly people seated around a table heaped with skulls. No mention was made of treasure.

In 1925, under the direction of Dr. W. Douglas Simpson, considerable excavations were carried out. No alarming discoveries were reported, but among the many interesting relics the famous silver gilt Kindrochit brooch was found. The walls of the main part of the castle were uncovered, but more is believed to exist below the shop. The remains of the old bridge across the Clunie were also uncovered.

John Taylor (1580-1659), the so-called Water Poet, was a Thames waterman, publican and pedestrian who, for a wager, set out from London to travel to Edinburgh, thence through the Scottish Highlands, carrying no money but relying on the hospitality of the people he encountered on the way. He was such a good-humoured, witty and friendly man that he made friends on his journey, and eventually completed his task.

He composed a vast amount of doggerel. In his *Short History of English Literature* George Saintsbury wrote, with some feeling, that Taylor received the very undeserved honour, denied to better men, of having all his works reprinted by the Spencer Society.

Apart from doggerel Taylor did leave us some interesting observations on his journeyings from London to Edinburgh and the Highlands. Of Braemar he had this to say:

"I came at night to the place I would be in the Brea of Mar, which is a large country, all composed of such mountaines, that Shooter's Hill, Gad's Hill, Hampstead Hill, Bridlip Hill, or Malvenes Hill, are but mole-hills by comparison, or like a liver, or a gizard under a capon's wing, in respect of the altitude of their tops, of perpendicularitie to their bottoms. There I saw Mount Ben Awne, with a furr'd mist upon his snowie head instead of a nightcap: for you must understand that the oldest man alive never saw but new snow was on the top of divers of those hills, both in summer as well as in winter."

The Great Forests of Badenoch

FAR back in the dim and distant past the umbrageous mass of the Caledonian Forest covered a large area of Badenoch and Rothiemurchus. It has been said that there is no more impressive place than the pine forest. It is full of suggestions, and quickens the mind; it lays a solemn spell on the spirit like the aisles of a cathedral: time no longer exists. It is marked by varying lights and shades by seasonal changes yet its aspect is perennially the same; changeless amid all the changes around it, the stillness is awe inspiring; unlike any other scene in nature. It is perhaps less the solitude than a mysterious presence, almost a supernatural influence. It is vividly described by Goethe in the 'Ballad of the Erl King' — the peculiar spirit or supernatural feeling of the forest. The silence is expectant: it seems to breathe, become audible, and to press upon the soul. The cry of a bird breaks it momentarily, or sometimes the sound of the wind in the treetops. Sometimes a gentle sigh from far off, yet not a breath of wind or a leaf stirring. It comes nearer, waxes louder then an all pervading murmur: like the voice of a god, and it is easy to understand how the pine forest was peopled with the mysterious presence of Northern mythology. There is a sense of being watched without love or malice. You seem when most alone least lonely. You are attuned to the Spirit of the Forest.

When the King of Lochlann (probably Norway) visited the Highlands he was deeply impressed by the immensity of the Caledonian Forest which covered large tracts of the Highlands. The trees were of enormous girth for the species, and some are said to have been twelve feet in circumference. So impressed was the King of Lochlann that when he returned home he was obsessed with recollections of the great forest he had seen and kept comparing them with his own, by comparison, scrubby woodlands.

His envy continued to grow, and to such an extent that in a fit of rage he called up a great monster said to have been his *muime* (step-mother) who was of enormous size. She had the head of a woman, the body of a whale and the wings of a eagle. She was bidden by the King to destroy all the forests in the Highlands so that he might be at peace with himself. The *muime* decided that the best way to achieve this was by fire in early summer when spring winds had made the undergrowth tinder dry.

When the time came she flew far above the clouds carrying a huge load of fire in her belly which first she dropped over the Sutherland Forests. Meanwhile the King of Lochlann raised a strong wind which fanned the flames, and drove them southwards through Ross-shire, Inverness and Moray, leaving behind a desert.

On the fire swept towards Glenmore, Rothiemurchus and Badenoch, and all attempts to stop the tide of destruction were unavailing. But a wise man of Kingussie was the saviour of the surrounding forests which were of such value to the people, both in the shape of timber for building and fuel, and also for their stock. When a council of the people gathered to discuss what action might be taken to arrest the approaching flames the wise one, a hunter whose voice was seldom heard in council, suddenly rose and said, "If you will obey me I promise to save the forests."

They agreed to do as they were bidden, and he ordered them to gather all their stock together, and drive the ewes, cows and mares to the east side of the Spey; the lambs, calves, and foals to the west bank. When the people had done this there was of course a tremendous uproar of baaing, bleating, mooing, and neighing. It was so loud that it reached the ears of the *muime*, who, full of curiosity, put her head through the screen of cloud to see what was going on, and this is precisely what the hunter had anticipated. His gun was already loaded with a home made silver bullet and, quickly taking aim, he shot the *muime* through the eye and she immediately fell to earth stone dead.

In an instant a dead calm set in and the flames were quickly brought under control, but what of the *muime*? It looked as if her decomposing corpse was to prove as big a problem as when she was alive, for she was far too big to bury and the people feared a plague might arise, but another saviour came quickly on the scene. It was soon noticed that swarms of insects began converging upon the *muime*'s corpse. Such insects, some red, some black, had never been seen in Badenoch. Soon all that remained of the *muime* was clean white bones, but the ants lingered and they it is said were the ancestors of the busy ants that today build their cities in the fir woods of Glenmore, Rothiemurchus and Badenoch.

The forests were again threatened, for tradition has it that Mary, Queen of Scots was so inflamed by a story that, on his return home from some sojourn, the Marquis of Huntly had enquired about the welfare of the forests before asking about the welfare of his Queen that she ordered the woods to be burned. She even took up station personally on a hill in Glenfeshie, ever after called *Sron na Barunn* (The Queen's Nose) to see that her orders were carried out. Fortunately, most of the woods escaped harm.

Over the years, and up to recent times, there have been many disastrous fires in the Forests of Abernethy, Glenmore and Rothiemurchus; some undoubtedly caused by careless picnickers or discarded cigarette ends and some by broken glass. Vandalism may have been suspected in a few. Present day organisation and modern fire fighting equipment provides a greater sense of security for the Forests.

Floating Timber Down the Spey

THE transport of timber by water was such a saga in the history of more than one river in the Cairngorms that it must now surely qualify as one of the legends of the district. The roads were little better than rough rutted tracks, and transport was slow and costly; transport by water was relatively simple, cheap and swift.

Winter sport activities and other recreations in upper Strathspey, and particularly in Glenmore and Rothiemurchus, recalled tales that the author's grandfather used to recount of the animated scenes in the forests, and of his own involvement in the work.

The destruction of the ancient forests, the Great Wood of Caledon, commenced for various reasons as far back as A.D.800 and exerted probably one of the greatest influences of man on the history of the Highlands. It continued during the fifteenth and sixteenth centuries, and up to the end of the eighteenth century.

After the collapse of the 1715 Rebellion impetus was given to the destruction by some of the Highland Chiefs who adopted English ways, and a higher standard of living. Large areas of forests were sold at ridiculous prices to unscrupulous speculators from the south for ship building and smelting, etc. The York Building Company acquired forfeited estates for next to nothing, and exploited their timber resources ruthlessly. In 1728 Sir James Grant sold 60,000 trees for the incredibly low sum of £7,000 or 2/4d per tree, probably in the region of a farthing per cubic foot.

The denudation of the forests continued until about 1850 when iron was introduced for ship building, and importations of foreign timber increased. The home timber trade declined, floating became a subject for reminiscences, and the remnants of the forest remained quiet until the 1914-18 Great War when the Canadian Forestry Corps arrived and added to the folly of denudation.

In the last War further inroads were made on the scanty reserves. There were in addition some devastating fires, and as a result of this and browsing by deer, sheep, rabbits and hares, natural regeneration was negligible. Today, largely due to the decline in the deer population, and the absence of serious forest fires, natural regeneration has increased to an encouraging degree.

If the ruthless exploitation had a single saving grace it was the employment in the logging and floating industry in otherwise extremely lean times, however short-sighted and unintelligent the policy was.

The River Spey was, until the construction of the Highland and Speyside Railways in 1863, of considerable economic importance to the district, and when its advantages as a means of transport were realised hundreds of local men in the parishes of Badenoch, Rothiemurchus and Abernethy were provided with employment, and an improved standard of living.

Three hundred years ago such was the abundance of first quality fir in these parishes and in Mar, and the difficulties encountered in finding a market for it that an annual payment of 1/8d. and one pound of tobacco entitled a native to cut as much timber for his own use as he could handle. But by the middle of the eighteenth century the price had risen steeply to 3/4½d. per tree, and the big timber merchants arrived from the south to exploit the riches of the forests.

To make planks and boards the local people first split the logs with wedges, then dressed them with axe and adze. Until its demolition a room in Castle Grant was floored with deals made in this way, and the adze marks were clearly visible. This was a very wasteful method of conversion, and it was succeeded by the laborious sawpit where the logs lay over a pit and were sawn to requirement by two men with a long saw, one man above, and the other down in the pit. This in turn was superseded by the more efficient single sawbench and circular saw.

Around 1738 part of Glenmore Forest was sold by the Duke of Gordon to Osborne and Dodsworth of Hull for a sum variously claimed as £10,000 and £20,000. Clear felling was restricted to one-fifth of the total timbered area, and only trees of a certain girth at breast height were to be cut, but no doubt there would have been some laxity in the observance of this clause in the Conditions of Sale. The area clear felled was approximately two hundred acres, yielding about 400,000 cubic feet. Today the value would be in the region of £2,400,000. Prior to the sale, Patrick Grant, an uncle of Sir John Peter Grant, the 7th Chief of the Rothiemurchus Grants, was offered Glenmore, wood, mountain, glen and loch for the sum of £10,000 but he declined it is a dear bargain. The sale of timber in Rothiemurchus Forest on a large scale did not commence until 1805.

During the twenty-two years of their operations, the Hull Company made enormous profits, despite mismanagement. When they first arrived in Glenmore they were greeted with hostility by the natives, and a local bard denounced their operations scornfully in Gaelic verse, a passage from which reads:

> Yonder's the little glen, kindly and sweet,
> Haunt of the full-grown harts,
> My curse on the bands of men that
> Have robbed it of its glory.
> Now, instead of the song of birds,
> And the murmur of deer in the thicket,
> Our ears are stunned by the crash
> Of falling trees and the clamours
> Of the Sassenach.

When felling and logging operations commenced it was an animated scene in the forest where the work was organised in four phases by Duncan Mcintosh, a local forester, who was in overall charge of the work for Osborne and Dodsworth.

Before work commenced at first light the fellers, draggers,

and loggers had their "morning", a gill of neat whisky. This was provided by young lads who went round the squads ladling out the drams with a horn gill measure from little casks on their backs. These casks contained a firkin or quarter anker of spirits, i.e. about 2½ gallons. Another measure was provided during the twenty-minute mid-day break, and this was sipped along with bannocks and cheese, the staple lunch in those days. Another gill was consumed at the end of the day's work.

Wood cutting was traditional in certain families in Strathspey and still is, and these men, like their forefathers, were highly skilled in felling, snedding and cross-cutting the trees to the best advantage and requirements. When a "face" had been felled and cross-cut into logs, the draggers hauled the logs to the banks of the Spey tributaries with garrons, the Luinneag flowing out of Loch Morlich, the Beannaidh from Loch Eanaich and the Milton Burn from Loch an Eilean. At the outfall from these lochs artificial embankments were constructed, and fitted with heavy sluice gates. When a desirable water level was reached, by ponding back the water, a sluiceman was despatched the night previous to a "run" so that the gates would be opened in good time for the flood water to reach the waiting loggers by first light. These embankments are still visible, and remnants of the sluice gates were to be found quite recently. One of these journeys ended in tragedy when Alan Grant, the Rothiemurchus sluiceman, made his way up Glen Eanaich in a fierce storm of wind and sleet. He succeeded in opening the gates, but died of exposure at his post.

Logging was an exciting event in the lives of the local men who were unfit to work through age or disability. With the women and children they gathered on the scene from the surrounding countryside when they were advised by bush telegraph that a "run" was imminent. Duncan Mcintosh often dined at the Doune, the seat of the Grants of Rothiemurchus, and usually contrived to call before a "run" so that those of the Grant family who wished to spectate were alerted in good time.

When the flood water arrived the loggers, working like beavers, poled the stacked logs on the banks into the rushing water. The youngest and most agile, each supplied with a cant hook or "clip", a long pole with a hook at the end, manoeuvred the logs, leaping from rock to rock, or rock to stump, and sometimes riding the logs. This exuberant band guided their charges downstream with whoops of excitement, sometimes falling into the water with suitable, or unsuitable, Gaelic expletives, or replying to the banter of their companions and spectators with great humour. Soakings did not seem to daunt them even though the water must sometimes have been freezing cold. On occasion fatal accidents occurred, and sometimes there were log jams. It was a serious and expensive business when hundreds of logs piled up interlocking in utter confusion, and many hard days of labour and considerable danger were entailed in clearing the jams. It is not recorded that explosives were used for this purpose.

The sawmills with circular saws which superseded the primitive sawpits were erected as near as possible to the felled timber which was converted into planks, and these were carted down to the Spey for rafting. The practice fell into disuse when it was found to be more economical to float the logs down the tributaries to the Spey, and convert them there in a large double mill. Some of the streams carried the logs straight into the Spey, while in others the logs were allowed to drift into lochans. Here light rafts of some of the logs were constructed, and paddled to small sawmills on the banks. The remaining logs were coaxed back to the main stream, thence to the Spey. These mills were also disbanded in time on economic grounds.

With regard to the whisky issues, an amusing story is told involving the Lady of Grant. It was the practice if a man, woman or child arrived at the logging scene with a message for one of the crews that they also received the traditional gill. On one occasion a logger's wife arrived with a child in her arms, and another trotting at her heels. When handed her quota she took a long pull then gave a sip to each child. Mrs. Grant, who was nearby, said to the little trotter, "My

257

goodness, child, doesn't it bite you?" "Ay, my Lady", he replied, "but I like the bite."

When the logs and planks reached the Spey another very important crew took command — the floaters. Timber is said to have been floated down the Spey from the end of the 15th century. The first rafts were made up of eight logs lashed together with horse hair ropes. Ahead of the raft a man in a *curach* or *coracle*, a small skiff made of wattle and bullock's hide, guided the cargo while men on the banks, holding ropes tied to the raft, controlled the speed and course through rocks and shoals. Methods had improved by the end of the 18th century, and rafts as big as the river could take were being sent down.

The floaters were specialists. They were not normally natives, although a few local men, including Donald Macpherson, the author's grandfather, did take part in floating for a time. The principal floaters were recruited from families in the Ballindalloch area, about 25 miles downstream from Aviemore.

Floating had been a tradition in several families for generations, and the principal floater of the day was called the "Admiral of the Spey". Two Grant families had the honour of guiding the first rafts down the Spey from Aviemore to Garmouth on the Moray Firth, a distance of about 60 miles. On the return journey the *curachs*, along with other gear, were carried on the men's backs. A notable floater was *Alasdair Mór a' Churaich* (Big Alasdair of the Curach). Another was Duncan Grant of Tulchan, a boy of 18 who, according to tradition, carried his *curach* the 600 miles to London to engage in a race with one of the small sailing craft on the Thames, in order to uphold the boast of his Chief. On a visit to London the Chief of the Grant commented admiringly to an English friend on the great variety of sailing craft on the Thames. In disparaging tones his friend replied, "You have, I suppose, nothing like that on your puny Spey." Nettled, the Chief retorted, "I have on the Spey a subject who, in a boat of bullock's hide, could outstrip the fastest of your craft." A wager was offered and taken, and a messenger was sent off to young Grant ordering him to come to London with his *curach* as quickly as possible.

It is not recorded how long the journey took, but Grant duly arrived and the race took place amidst great excitement from the spectators lining the banks. Oars and sail were pitted against him but Duncan outstripped them all, much to his Chief's delight, and the chagrin of the loser. The spectators, appreciative of the boy's courage and skill, showered so many gold coins on him that his bonnet was nearly full. But Duncan disdained to accept their largesse, and handed the bounty to his Chief with the request that it should be given to the Lady of Grant. Probably it was used for the common good of the Rothiemurchus people.

On a level part of the river bank just below where the old bridge crossed the Spey at Aviemore the floaters had their quarters, a large wooden hut with a fire on a stone hearth in the middle, and a hole in the roof to allow at least some of the smoke to escape. The floor was strewn with heather for bedding. And here each night after a day in the river soaked to the waist they lay down to sleep wrapped in their plaids, feet to the fire, half stupefied with whisky, and enveloped in a cloud of smoke, steam and whisky fumes. But who would grudge them the whisky! They were a hardy breed, and appeared to take no hurt except in old age when they suffered from rheumatism.

There was a high degree of skill in constructing the huge cigar-shaped rafts so that on the long journey to the sea the risk of disintegrating in rough waters would be minimal. Certainly over the years the passage had been improved by blasting and clearing rocks, but hazards remained despite the floater's long experience of shoals, currents and hidden rocks. The logs were bored at each end with an auger and iron eye bolts were hammered in. Twisted wattles were passed through the eyes and round the logs so that any given number of logs could be bound together until the whole cargo was consolidated. Later chains were used to rack the logs together. On this base the deals, planks, and battens from the sawmills were decked until the full complement was aboard and bound. Two rude gears for huge oars, one at each end, completed the raft. The journey downstream was a wet one, for at every lurch the raft shipped water. The oars, fashioned locally, were the perquisite of the Lady of Grant who received "oar money". They sold for 2/6d each, and in one season she received the handsome sum of £40.

At the first sign of a spate preparations were made for the sixty mile journey down river. The current bore them along at a rapid pace, the rafts being controlled by two men with the huge oars at the bow and stern, and preceded by men in *curachs* as guides.

The journey to Garmouth, where the timber was used for shipbuilding, usually took a day. The most expert floaters would make the journey to Garmouth in 12 hours, and return on foot as far as Rothiemurchus by nightfall. The number of tenants in the Parishes of Abernethy, and Kincardine alone employed in the industry was about 90, and their earnings were often more than enough to cover their rents. In 1839, 91 tenants earned £452 and in 1840, 95 received £636. Seventy pounds per annum was a considerable income for a man in 1840.

A centre nearer the mouth of the Spey became more desirable as business prospered, and Kingstone village was born. The name derived from the Hull Company's headquarters at Kingston-upon-Hull. The Company built 47 ships with a gross tonnage of 19,000 tons, and the work was commemorated by presenting a huge memorial plank of Glenmore fir, six feet wide, to the Duke of Gordon. On it was a brass plate with the following inscription - "In the year 1783 William Osbourne, Esq., Merchant of Hull, purchased of the Duke of Gordon the forest of Glenmore, the whole of which he cut down in the space of 22 years, and built during that time, at the mouth of the river Spey, where never was built before, 47 sail of ships of upwards of 19,000 tons burthen. The largest of them of 1,050 tons, three others but little inferior in size, are now in the service of His Majesty and the Honourable East India Company. This undertaking was completed at the expense (for labour only) of above £70,000. To His Grace, the Duke of Gordon, this plank is offered as a specimen of the growth of one of the trees in the above Forest by his Grace's most obedient servant W. Osbourne, Hull, 1806".

The plank was on display at Gordon Castle for many years. In 1877, by kind permission of the Duke of Gordon and at the request of Sir Robert Christison, Bart., the plank was on exhibition in the National Museum of Science and Art, Edinburgh. According to Sir Robert, "the plank was 5'7" wide at the bottom. The tree must have been 19'0" girth at the bottom of the plank and 16'0" at the top, 6'3" higher up I can make out 243 layers on one radius; seven are wanting in the centre and seven years must be added for the growth of the tree to the place of measurement. Hence the tree must have been 260 years old. The outer layers on the radius are so wide that it must have been growing at a goodly rate when it was cut down.

Some years ago when the author sought confirmation from the Factor at Gordon Castle that it was still there, he learned with dismay that no one on the Estate had any knowledge of the existence of such a plank. Unremitting search followed and finally, after six years, it was traced to the Forestry Department of the University of Aberdeen.

It is not, of course, strictly correct that Messrs. Osbourne and Dodsworth cut the whole Forest of Glenmore.

The great social event of the year for the timber crews and floaters, and their families was the Floaters' Ball, held annually about Christmas at the Rothiemurchus Home Farm. Everyone concerned in the forest work and floating was invited. In began early in the day with shinty matches which continued until dusk, when the men repaired to the barn for a feast of beef and mutton. The women were served more genteely with tea in the grieve's house. Then the dancing commenced in the hay and straw lofts, and the upper floor of the granary. Two sets of fiddlers supplied the music, and there were copious libations of whisky punch made in the wash tubs. The illumination was by tallow candles. When a young man led a girl to her place in the reel he kissed her before the dance commenced in traditional manner, she holding up her face quite frankly for the customary salute. In Scots this was called "preeing her mou'". The Napoleonic Wars created a demand for timber, but in the aftermath the price of timber slumped. Floating flourished until about 1850 but, with the introduction of iron for shipbuilding and the import of foreign timber, it declined, and almost died when the big cut ended in Rothiemurchus Forest.

About 1860 much of the remaining timber on Rothiemurchus was felled to provide sleepers for the Highland Railway.

There has been appreciable natural regeneration of the old stock. In addition, extensive planting had been carried out in Glenmore (the Queen's Forest) over the last fifty years by the Forestry Commission, and in Abernethy Forest by Seafield Estate. Unfortunately, little planting has been carried out in Rothiemurchus Forest, and most of the existing cover is part of the old forest, and part natural regeneration.

How the York Building Company came to Strathspey in the first place is difficult to say. They were a remarkably daring and enterprising Company and may well have scented huge profits in the reports of Aaron Hill, the poet, who had a great conceit of his own gifts for literature and speculation. Hill travelled widely, and wrote a number of books. He was a socialite who was accepted in the highest circles in London and Edinburgh, and he might possibly have met in those cities the Chief of Grant and others, and learned from them about the vast timber resources of their lands. Quite possibly he had seen a report dated 1750 by Captain John Mason who, on behalf of the Commissioners of the Navy, held a forty year Lease of Abernethy Forest.

Whatever the truth of these speculations he certainly journeyed North in 1706, and wrote such a glowing report about the magnitude of the forests ripe for exploitation to the York Building Company that they immediately set about obtaining a Licence to Trade. In 1728 the Royal Licence was granted, "...to trade in goods, wares and merchandise of the growth and produce of that part of the Kingdom." By an indenture dated 5th January 1728 between Sir James Grant and the Company 60,000 fir trees of the best quality lying in the Forests of Abernethy and Kincardine were purchased. They were empowered, "...to fell, sell, transport and to their own use and behoof apply the said trees at their own charge and risque within seventeen years and that every tree wounded by them shall be deemed one of the number hereby sold". The price agreed was £7,000, or approximately one shilling and one penny per tree. Even for that time it appears a poor price per tree.

The Company immediately took possession, and made a bold start. They rented Coulnakyle and entertained on a lavish scale. Aaron Hill was riding high on the crest of a wave of anticipated prosperity and quoted his own lines frequently with glowing confidence:

> High on the mountains of her northern shore
> The gummy pine shall shed her pitchy store;
> Tall firs, which useless have long ago grown,
> Shall freight the seas and visit lands unknown
> Till the checked sons of Norway's timbered state
> Learn love by force while we disarm their hate,

Aaron Hill also hinted at "subterranean riches" rivalling those of Mexico and Peru. His dreams outpaced his common sense; letters to his wife were written from the "Golden Groves of Abernethy". Captain Burt, one of the gentlemen closely involved in the venture, and a more practical type, predicted that none of the trees would pay for the price of felling, extraction over rocks and bogs, and transport by rocky rivers to the coast, "as I believe the York Building Company will find in the conclusion." Prophetic words!

Colonel Horsey, another of the gentlemen involved, and Aaron Hill had by now their sights on another local asset - iron ore. There was, they understood, large quantities of the ore in the Lecht Hills, and they conceived a scheme whereby the iron would be transported to Abernethy and smelted where there was an abundance of wood. They raced whole-heartedly but blindly into this new venture. Works were erected on the River Nethy; smelting furnaces at Balnagowan and a forging mill near the Causer where, to this day, the foundation beams, cross-braces and large headed iron nails may still be seen in the river bed. Some distance below the Dell of Abernethy lay the Iron Mill Croft, and it is believed that the Company had a smelting plant in the vicinity. No trace of it could be found until, in the Great Flood of 1829, a channel was scoured through the croft, and the framework of a gangway across the river with a platform was exposed. This was assumed to be the foundation of the Mill House. Houses were built to accommodate the labourers, and perhaps over fifty men and one hundred and twenty garrons were engaged in transporting the ore in panniers from the Lecht Hills. Meanwhile many more were employed in felling and extracting the trees, and working in the sawmills which the Company had built. Aaron Hill quickly improved the traditional method of floating timber down the Spey, by devising solidly built rafts steered by two men with long oars, one at the front and one behind.

These activities went on for some years, but Captain Burt's predictions were looming ominously near. The Company's lavish expenditure was noted by the Rev. John Grant in the *Old Statistical Account*: "Their extravagances of every kind ruined themselves and corrupted others. They used to display their vanity by bonfires, tar barrels and opening hogsheads of brandy to the country people by which five of them died in one night. They had a Commissary for provisions and forage at a handsome salary; and in the end went off in debt to the proprietors and the company." The Company were unable to fulfil their engagements, rents went unpaid, debts and difficulties mounted daily until finally there was complete collapse. By 1745 the Company was in liquidation.

It must be said, however, that the activities were beneficial in a number of respects; new knowledge and skills were acquired by the local people, and they created many lasting improvements. They carried out roadworks which improved communications, the sawmills they erected were far in advance of the traditional sawpits and single sawbenches. The rafts they devised were, as already mentioned, a great improvement on the traditional types, and they did clear a passage in the Spey by blasting the rocks which had previously created so much difficulty for the rafts.

Actions were raised against the Company in the Court of Session but little or nothing in favour of the debtors appears to have emerged from them, and silence again reigned in the forests where there had been so much activity and clamour. The vast enterprise was dead. The last recorded float was in 1899 when timber was guided down the Spey from Loch Morlich after a devastating fire round the shores of the Loch. But there was a float on some special occasion much later, and Lewis Grant of Revoan was specially consulted because of his unique knowledge in the art of floating. During the 1914-18 Great War the Canadian Forestry Corps, who were encamped in Glenmore, removed 76,000 trees from Glenmore and transported them to Aviemore by light railway. This was in theory a selective felling or group felling to ensure natural regeneration of the old forest. But the Canadians were not very fussy. Their huts and the flumes which were used for floating the timber down were to be seen for a good many years after. Traces may still be there.

Again in the 1939-45 Great War about 200 acres were felled producing somewhere in the region of 400,000 cubic feet.

In 1960, on account of local objections, the Forestry Commission had to suspend the clean cut of 20 acres of 200 year old firs near Glenmore Lodge.

Even today the forests are endangered by a surprising lack of foresight, as illustrated by a press report on March 1984 in which the Royal Society for the Protection of Birds protested at the cutting down of 100 acres of unique pine forests at Abernethy, despite their internationally recognised importance for wildlife by the Government's Nature Conservancy Council.